THE FARMER'S BOY

THE FARMER'S BOY

The Story of a Suffolk Poet
Robert Bloomfield, his life and poems
1766 - 1823

by

WILLIAM WICKETT and NICHOLAS DUVAL

TERENCE DALTON LIMITED
LAVENHAM   .   SUFFOLK
1971

Published by
TERENCE DALTON LIMITED
S B N 900963 28 X

Chapter head illustrations
from engravings in an early
edition of The Farmer's Boy

Printed in Great Britain at
The Lavenham Press Limited
Lavenham   Suffolk

Contents

Acknowledgements ... 8

Chapter 1   The Early Years   9

Chapter 2   The Farmer's Boy   19

Chapter 3   His Love Poems   37

Chapter 4   The Sea and the River Wye   43

Chapter 5   Move to Bedfordshire   53

Epilogue   67

The Works of Robert Bloomfield

The Farmer's Boy   Spring   70

     Summer   80

     Autumn   90

     Winter   100

The Horkey   110

To My Old Oak Table   116

Richard and Kate or Fair Day — A Suffolk Ballad   120

Barnham Water   125

Market Night   127

Song for a Highland Drover — Returning from England   ..   129

The Fakenham Ghost — A Ballad   131

Irish News — *Tune: The Yorkshireman*   134

Journey down the Wye — The Coracle   135

     Gleaner's Song   136

The Man in the Moon   137

On Repairing a Miniature Bust of Buonaparte for Mrs. Palmer   138

Sonnet to 15 Gnats Dancing in the Sunbeams on January 3   ..   139

From a Swallow in the South of France to an English Robin — Letter   140

Hob's Epitaph   141

Hazelwood Hall   Glee for Three Voices   142

     Extract from Act II Scene II   ..   142

     Betty's Song   144

The Vale of Fakenham   144

Index of Illustrations

(i)   Robert Bloomfield

(ii)   Elizabeth Bloomfield (Robert's mother)

(iii)   Sapiston Church

(iv)   Triangle House, Sapiston

(v)   The Grange, Sapiston

(vi)   Ford and water mill, Sapiston

(vii)   Bloomfield's cottage, Honington

(viii)   The old oak table

(ix)   Engraving of Honington Church

(x)   Honington Church in 1971

(xi)   Troston Hall

(xii)   Edward Jenner

(xiii)   Capel Lofft

(xiv)   Euston Hall

(xv)   Church in Euston Park

(xvi)   Memorial plaque to Trouncer

(xvii)   Site of Bardwell Fair

(xviii)   Gateway to Euston Park

(xix)   Fakenham Ghost — the drove way and stile

(xx)   Lankets Grove

(xxi)   Barnham Water

(xxii)   Grave headstone, Elizabeth and Isaac William Bloomfield, Honington

(xxiii)   Grave headstone Robert Bloomfield, Campton.

A Shepherd's Boy, he seeks no better name

Motto on the title page of the edition of The Farmer's Boy illustrated
by Nesbitt and published in 1800.

Acknowledgement

The Authors wish to acknowledge the help they have received from many people and organisations. In particular they would like to thank Mr. Neville Blackburne; Rev. H. H. Bloomfield; the Cambridge Institute of Education; Mr. A. R. Edwardson, Curator, Moyses' Hall Museum, Bury St. Edmunds; The Houghton Library, Harvard University, Massachusetts, U.S.A.; Suffolk Fair Magazine; Surrey County Librarian, Mr. Robert F. Ashby; West Suffolk County Archivist; West Suffolk Newspapers Limited.

I   The Early Years.

It was at Honington in Suffolk that the poet Robert Bloomfield was born on December 3rd, 1766, in a cottage near the village church.

His parents, George and Elizabeth Bloomfield, were married at Sapiston on June 1st 1755 but set up their first home close by at Fakenham. It was not long before they moved to a cottage in Honington which George's father had bought and where George himself had been brought up. They were a highly respected young couple of some rustic refinement and high moral standards. Mr. Narrowback and Mrs. Prim, as they were affectionately known by the villagers, were soon accepted into the local community which managed to draw a living from the kindly land bordering the Blackbourne river. This stream flowed down from Ixworth past Thorpe and Bardwell and the Duke of Grafton's stately home at Euston to join the Ouse at Thetford. They were peasant folk in that they belonged to the country and they were poor. The father, who was a nimble little fellow barely five feet in height and very fragile, was a tailor and his wife, a Miss Manby of Brandon, was, as her nickname suggests, very 'prim and proper'. But she was also hard-working and courageous, with great strength of character as the story of her life very clearly shows.

In 1767, when Robert was not yet a year old, his father was stricken with the smallpox and died leaving his widow with a family of six children to bring up on her own. Of these the eldest, George, was only just eleven, and it was he who, years afterwards, told Robert the gruesome story of their father's burial by the dim light of the sexton's lantern at midnight in Honington churchyard. Robert vividly describes the scene in his *Good Tidings From The Farm*.

"Midnight beheld the close of all his pain,
His grave was closed when midnight came again;
No bell was heard to toll, no funeral prayer,
No kindred bow'd, no wife, no children there;
Its horrid nature could inspire a dread
That cut the bonds of custom like a thread.
The humble church-tower higher seemed to show,
Illumin'd by the trembling light below;
The solemn night-breeze struck each shiv'ring cheek,
Religious reverence forbade to speak:
The starting sexton his short sorrow chid
When the earth murmured on the coffin lid,
And falling bones and sighs of holy dread
Sounded a requiem to the silent dead."

The family struggled on and Mrs. Bloomfield, besides keeping a Dame's School, was obliged to spin wool in order to maintain her children. Robert appears to have been very happy as a small boy growing up under the eye of his doting mother, whose favourite he seems to have been. He was a precocious child who learnt to read almost as soon as he could talk, and he writes in later years of those "sunny days that ever haunt my dreams". They sang little ditties together as they worked, Robert helping his mother to 'twirl' the spindles. In addition to the education which she could give him, she managed to send him to The Senior Clerk to the Blackbourne Magistrates, a Mr. Rodwell, who kept a school at Ixworth,* for instruction in what we should now call creative writing or composition. For three months, in 1777, he plodded along the rough road by the stream for his lessons there. Among the books which he read at this time were *Goody-Two-Shoes* and *The History of Jack-The-Giant-Killer*, still popular with children to-day. In those days books of all kinds were hard to come by, as were also the skills required in order to read them, but Robert was fortunate, at least, in having access to two of his mother's treasured volumes—The Bible and *The Pilgrim's Progress*. His grandfather, Mr. Robin Manby of Brandon, who had given his mother something of an education, was anxious that she in turn should

---

*The house in which Mr. Rodwell taught his pupils still stands in North Street.

10

see to it that her own children could at least read and write. Accordingly he allowed her, and them, the use of the few books which were his, among them Thomas Gray's *Elegy written in a Country Church-yard*, as well as Goldsmith's *The Deserted Village* and Watts' *Hymns*. It is hardly likely that Robert was able to comprehend any of them properly, but it is significant that his most famous work, *The Farmer's Boy*, was written entirely in the same style, and in the rhyming couplets of iambic pentameter, used by Goldsmith.

After six years of widowhood Mrs. Bloomfield re-married at Ampton in 1773, a widower called John Glover, whose wife had died the previous December.

Soon afterwards the two eldest sons, George and Nathaniel, went off to London to work, the one as a ladies' shoemaker and the other as a tailor. For a while this eased the tension in the home somewhat, but the second marriage also produced children and the little house was again strained to capacity. By the time Robert was eleven, it became necessary for him to begin work. His grandfather Manby died at Little Fakenham,* where he had moved from Brandon, and the financial help he had been able to give had ceased. But where was he to work? There was little choice really for, although he was of a studious nature, the expense of an academic career was out of the question. He was already showing signs of becoming a great lover of the countryside. It is a pity we do not have any of the little sketches he made at that early age, of the birds and the animals he loved and the trees with which he was so well acquainted. As a result of a family conference his uncle by marriage, Mr. William Austin, offered help. This kindly gentleman farmed a considerable acreage of land at Sapiston, and, although he had a large family of his own to consider, he agreed to take young Robert to live with them and share their way of life in his farmhouse, close to the Church and the watermill. Here he worked as a farmer's boy in the farmyard and the fields, receiving only food and lodging and a little spending-money in return for his work, his mother having undertaken to provide him with clothes, which was as much as she was able to do. Robert was extremely happy attending the workmen, minding the sheep, fetching the cows, scaring the birds and doing all kinds of work around the farm. It was during the nearly four years spent here that he gained

---

*The authors have encountered confusion in the minds of some readers of the works of Bloomfield in which Fakenham occurs. This village, Little Fakenham, is shown on Ordnance Survey Maps (One inch Sheet 136) on the A1088 between Euston and Honington. It should not be confused with its apparently better known namesake, the Fakenham in Norfolk.

the intimate knowledge of rural life and the customs and habits of the people which later was to provide the substance for his master-piece *The Farmer's Boy*, which was to take the literary world by storm in the years to come. But he was, like his father, of short and fragile build and strangely unsuited for any hard work on the farm. By the time he was fourteen it became obvious that he would never develop the physique to enable him to take his proper place with the other workers as he grew into manhood, for he was still small and weakly despite good food and fresh air. So Mr. Austin had to advise his mother to try and find him some less strenuous employment elsewhere. He had in mind one of the trades practised by his elder brothers, both of whom were already in London, and suggested that she should see what they were willing to do about it. Both George and Nathaniel responded most willingly, the former offered to take his young brother under his protection and teach him his trade and the latter agreed to clothe him.

On Friday, June 29th 1781, Mrs. Glover took him up by stage-coach to London and gave him into George's hands charging him, as he valued a mother's blessing, to watch over him, to set good examples for him, and never to forget that he had lost his father. Later in life, when recalling the excitement he experienced on leaving home, he said, "I well remember the palpitation of my heart on receiving George's proposal to come to town, and how incessantly I thought of the change I was going to experience, selling my smock frock for a shilling to Sam Shelver's boy and slily washing my best hat in the horse-pond to give it gloss fit to appear in the meridian of London." His brother George also recorded his own impressions of Robert's arrival there in these words: "I have in my mind's eye a little boy, not bigger than boys generally are at twelve years old. When I met him and his mother at the Inn* he strutted before us just as he came from keeping sheep, hogs etc... his shoes fill'd full of stumps in the heels. He, looking about him, slipt up...his nails were unus'd to a flat pavement. I remember viewing him as he scamper'd up...how small he was. Little thought I that little fatherless boy would be one day known and esteem'd by the most learned, the most respected, the wisest and the best men of the Kingdom."

George, now twenty-three, worked with four other men in a garret at Mr. Simm's of No 7, Pitcher's Court in Bell Alley, quite near Great Coleman Street in the City of London and not far from Guildhall. It was here that young Robert was to sleep and work. Life was strange for him in many ways. There were only two turn-up beds for the

---

*In Bishopsgate Street.

six of them and they were not the soft cosy type that he had been used to at home. But he soon settled in and adapted himself to his new surroundings with remarkable ease. He was happy and popular with the men with whom he worked "fetching and carrying" for them and reading aloud to them yesterday's newspaper as they did their work; they in turn assisted him with his, and did something extra to make up for the time he had lost. Frequently in his reading he encountered unfamiliar words which he could not understand but this problem was solved when his brother came across an old tattered dictionary which he bought for fourpence from a bookstall. He rapidly gained a good knowledge of the English language and was able to read, understand and appreciate the speeches of such great orators as Burke, Fox and North. A few books came his way at this time, among them a *History of England*, a *British Traveller* and a *Geography*, all of which came in weekly numbers, paid for by the workmen. George took the *London Magazine* and this Robert read avidly; it was in the Poet's Corner of this publication that his first poetical effort, *The Village Girl*, was published, when he was only sixteen.

London at the end of the eighteenth century was a vile place by modern standards, but Robert was not corrupted by his environment and showed no interest in the gambling, cock-fighting, bull-baiting or fornication that went on there. Having been brought up by a pious mother in a Christian home he was able to stand up to the temptations which came his way, and preferred rather to seek relaxation in walks in the country. On Sunday mornings he frequently attended St Paul's Cathedral to worship. It is interesting to note that his cousin, Charles James Bloomfield, many years later, was enthroned there as the 119th Bishop of London. In his poem *To My Old Oak Table* he describes one of his visits to the Cathedral:

> "Beneath that vast gigantic dome we bow'd,
> That lifts its flaming cross above the cloud;
> Had gained the centre of the chequer'd floor;
> That instant with reverberating roar,
> Burst forth the pealing organ—mute we stood,
> The strong sensation boiling through my blood,
> Rose in a storm of joy, allied to pain,
> I wept and worshipp'd God, and wept again;
> And felt, amidst the fervour of my praise,
> The sweet assurances of better days."

But Sunday was also the day upon which George and Robert took their long walks into the surrounding countryside of Kent and Middlesex. It was after one of these rambles that they turned, by accident, into a dissenting Meeting-House in the Old Jewry where a certain Mr. Fawcett was lecturing. The place was crowded, and the brothers had to stand in the aisle. Robert was spellbound by the discourse, and returned week after week to listen to more of these lectures. From this famous preacher he soon learnt to accent what he called hard words and otherwise improved his powers of verbal expression. Occasionally he went to a debating society in The Coach-maker's Hall, but the speeches there savoured of the political and the malcontent and were not at all in keeping with his purposeful and peace-loving nature. He also went a few times to the Covent Garden Theatre, but this meant spending money, which he could not well afford. These were the only opportunities he had to learn from the great public speakers of his time but, with his phenomenal memory, he was able to retain for all time what was good and beautiful in all that he heard.

Thus the first two years of his exile passed happily by, but the regular letters which he wrote to his mother showed that at times he was homesick and longed for the quiet countryside. Whilst he was mastering the intricacies of his craft, he was also gaining an exceptional command of English. He was nearly seventeen when a man, subject to frequent epileptic fits, came to lodge in the house where he was. Because of the effect which the sight of this poor creature during his bouts of epilepsy had upon the sensitive boy, his brother decided that they must move away. They obtained fresh lodgings not far away in Blue Hart Court. Here Robert made the acquaintance of a remarkable Scotsman named James Kay, a native of Dundee, who was something of a scholar, and a rabid Calvinist. It was from him that he learnt about many of the poets, and it was from him that he was able to borrow, among others, Milton's *Paradise Lost*, Thomson's *Seasons* and novels of the day such as *Tristram Shandy*, *The Vicar of Wakefield*, and the *Castle of Otranto*. James Thomson, a Scottish poet born in 1700 and dying 48 years later, had written *The Seasons* which he divided into four parts; spring, summer, autumn, winter. This concept took Bloomfield's fancy and years later, when he wrote *The Farmer's Boy* he made use of the same idea. But there the similarity ends. The work was entirely original, and in Bloomfield's own simple and inimitable style. He took absolutely nothing from Thomson except, perhaps, the urge to write.

Back in Honington things were happening. In the autumn of 1783 the village had experienced a great fire in which no less than five 'double-dwellers', the Rectory, and a farm-house together with the out-buildings were destroyed in under an hour. Robert's mother fled from the home, also being used as a school, taking all her little pupils with her into the fields down the mill lane, together with the deeds of her house and a clock. Fortunately her dwelling escaped the flames and she was able to return safely to it. But her husband, John Glover, never recovered from the shock of it all, and died a month or two later. The studded doors from the Rectory were saved from the fire and today provide the main entrance to Honington Post Office.

Early in 1784 a dispute arose between the journeymen shoemakers and their employers as to whether anyone who had learned without serving an apprenticeship could follow the trade. Robert was not properly apprenticed, and therefore he and George who taught him, and Mr. Chamberlayne of Cheapside who employed them, were all involved. Prosecution by the Committee of The Lawful Crafts was threatened, and Robert, as usual peace-loving and fearful, begged to be allowed to withdraw from the storm that was arising, and to go home to Honington until it had passed and he could return once more to London to resume his work there. His previous employer and benefactor, Mr. Austin, realised how difficult it would be for his mother to take him into her home following her second husband's death and offered him a home for as long as it was necessary. This was to prove fortunate both for him and for the English language and literary heritage for here amid the fields and the countryside of his early youth he saw again the beauty of nature and added to the rich rural memories from which he was to draw so copiously whilst writing *The Farmer's Boy*. It was summer and he used to wander down by the Blackbourne out into the Fakenham wood and along to Euston, Barnham and Thetford. He frequently mentions The Grove, Lanket's Grove, which was a favourite resort for lovers, and where the wild strawberries grew in profusion. He was now eighteen, and the strong impulses of love were beginning to move in his veins. It was at this time that he fell in love with Nancy Bantock of Broadmere. Years afterwards he wrote a passionate poem recalling this happy time. He renewed his friendship with her when he came back to Honington in 1786, but on his next visit, two years later, he found that she had already married a local swain and was lost to him for ever.

At the end of the summer the dispute over apprenticeship had not been settled, but an arrangement had been made by which Robert

15

could go back to work in London. Mr. John Dudridge, George's landlord and a Freeman of the City, had agreed that the boy should be properly apprenticed to him at a token payment of five shillings, as a matter of form to meet the legal occasion, and that he would never enforce the terms of the indentures. This enabled Robert again to work with his brother until he became his equal in his craft and George then felt free to leave him. He set up in business on his own account at Bury St Edmunds, in his native Suffolk. Robert, now turned twenty, began to study music and learnt to play the violin; he also made and sold Aeolian harps,* which were very fashionable in those days. For these he developed quite an affection, which lasted to the end of his life. James Montgomery the Scottish poet, wrote "I saw him once at the *Shepherd and Shepherdess*, in London, and bespoke an Aeolian Harp of him." For a year or two he sought the companionship of his other brother, Nathaniel, and went down with him to Woolwich, where he became fascinated with the Dockyard and the Barracks. There he saw the launching of the battleship *The Boyne* and was able to admire, on the way, the observatory at Greenwich, where Flamstead had worked. He was present at the wedding of his brother to the sixteen-year-old Charlotte Noble, when it is thought that he met for the first time, his own future wife, Mary Anne Church, whose father was a boatbuilder in the Woolwich Dockyard. This comely young lady was no doubt a friend of Charlotte's, since they both hailed from Woolwich and were about the same age. Robert corresponded regularly with his brother, George, in Bury St Edmunds and in 1790 he wrote... "I have sold my fiddle and got me a wife." The wedding took place on December 12th 1790, and their first child, Hannah, was born the following year, at 14, Bell Alley, Coleman Street, not far from his old lodgings. They had only a first floor room with a garret above, up two flights of stairs. In these drear surroundings, with only a bed and a few sticks of furniture, including an old oak table† given them on their wedding day by father-in-law Church

---

*In Moyses' Hall Museum, Bury St. Edmunds, there is an Aeolian Harp made by Bloomfield.

†This old oak table, which having the top pivoted turns into a chair, is now in the Moyses' Hall Museum, and on it is the following inscription—
"This celebrated Old Oak Table and Chair was the property of Robert Bloomfield the poet on which he wrote with other poems (To My Old Oak Table). It afterwards became the property of Charles Bloomfield who lived at Honington in Suffolk— But being in difficulties was sold at auction at Bury St. Edmonds and was bought by a Mrs Best. Mrs Charles Tyler her daughter came posessed of it at her death. And when she left Thetford May 5 1875 gave it to me. Robert Bloomfield Died August 19th 1823.   Presented by the Marshall Family 1937."

16

they spent the next ten years. Robert then worked for a high-class ladies' shoemaker, a Mr. Davies of Lombard Street. Ill-health came to the father and mother and the children in turn, for by 1800 there were three—Hannah, Mary Anne and Charles. It was difficult to make ends meet, despite the rise in wages of the craftsmen during the middle 1790's. We have, by chance, a letter which Robert wrote to his father-in-law at the beginning of this period. It is in cheerful mood and Robert is looking to the future with ambition and hope following the birth of his first child Hannah.

It is one of the most interesting and revealing of his letters written in 1791 early in his married life and long before he became famous; in fact he was then contemplating setting up in the shoemaking business on his own account.

Wednesday night Dec 28 — 91

Hon Father,

It would have been a great pleasure to us both to have met you at Mr. Wyatt's this time, and we were only prevented by visitors, who came quite unexpected. You would have liked to have seen our little one; and I hope you will yet before long. We thank you for all your kindness, and as I am endeavouring to get into business for myself, I sincerely hope to have it in my power to entertain you better when you come. I have an undeniable chance. I have some good customers, and might have enough immediately to provide a genteel living for my wife and child, if I could take advantage of it soon. If I could get three months credit at my leather-cutters, for five or six pounds only, it would enable me to give credit to that amount, as my custom lies among such as are able and willing to improve it; but I am determined to carry it on as well as I can......

My Polly and child are in good health and I hope to hear from you soon; and remain yours, in duty and affection

Robert Bloomfield.

But his hopes were not immediately realised for—

"Soon came the days that tried a faithful wife,
The noise of children and the cares of life.
Then, midst the threatenings of a wintry sky,
That cough which blights the bud of infancy,
The dread of parents, rest's inveterate foe,
Came like a plague and turn'd my songs to woe."

The poem goes on to describe the sufferings mentally and physically that the family endured in these early days of marriage, the poet in particular being greatly afflicted with melancholia, headaches and rheumatism. When, however, he had regained his strength after some six or seven years, he began the composition of *The Farmer's Boy* among all the hubbub of a shoemaker's workshop and the general squalor of his surroundings.

2   The Farmer's Boy

It is amazing that he was able to produce such work in these circumstances. But his memory and imagination were so prodigious that nearly the whole poem was complete in his mind long before it was written down. The manuscript was finished on April 22nd 1798 and the search for a publisher began. It was first sent to Mr. Bent, publisher of *The Universal Magazine*, who kept it for about ten days and then sent it back by a grave, bookish-looking man who brusquely stated, "It doesn't suit." Then Bloomfield took it, himself, to Mr. Lane, "the wholesale novel manufacturer."

This aristocratic man did not care for the poet's appearance, and dismissed him with, "Poetry is quite out of my line." Mr. Dilly of The Poultry, who had recently published Clare Reeve's *The Old English Baron*, was not at all impressed and observed, "It needs revision, is not suitable etc. etc." And so it went the rounds and was shown to many people in turn—people of his own acquaintance and others outside his own circle, but it was seen by no-one capable of judging it nor by anyone who would admit that work of such outstanding literary merit could come from an uneducated or rather self-educated pauper-shoemaker. At last, by great good fortune and by the efforts of his brother, George, in Suffolk, it was passed to Mr. Capel Lofft, a Whig barrister and a magistrate, living at Troston Hall just three miles from Honington, who extended his patronage to the poet, read his manuscript, wrote the preface to the work and arranged for its publication, thus giving to the world a gem of pastoral poetical composition which might otherwise have been lost to posterity. He was a great philanthropist and radical and was also involved in the organisation of an appeal against the death sentence passed upon a servant girl Sarah Lloyd in 1802 for stealing goods worth but 40s from her employer in Bury after allowing two soldier friends into the house whilst her mistress was out. One of the signatories was the then Duke of Grafton, but Lofft went as far as to climb up into the tumbril which was taking the girl to her death at the Tayfen Meadows and harangue the crowd for a quarter of an hour. For his part in this episode he was struck off the roll of magistrates. He became Bloomfield's greatest admirer and friend. He never ceased to extol him, and it was through his good offices that many able and influential people in all walks of life and in many parts of the country and particularly in Suffolk became interested in his work and in his welfare, among them H.R.H. the Prince of Wales, the Duke of Grafton of Euston Hall, the Earl of Buchan, the Duke of York, Captain Bunbury of Livermere,* and the Shakespearian writer, Dr. Drake of Hadleigh.

The first edition of *The Farmer's Boy*† was published on March 1st 1800 by Messrs Vernor and Hood of The Poultry. A second edition followed very quickly, it being published simultaneously in London, Norwich and Bury St Edmunds. The demand was so great that a third edition was on sale before the end of the year, and a fourth early in 1801. By the time the seventh edition came in 1803 no less than 30,000 copies had been sold. Apart from arranging the publication of the poem, Mr. Lofft, in his preface says this, "My part has been this, and it has been a very pleasing one; to revise the MS making occasionally corrections with respect to the orthography, and sometimes in the grammatical construction. The corrections in point of Grammar

---

*Captain Sir Charles Bunbury of Great Barton and Livermere was a man of many interests, among them an appreciation of the Arts and a love of good literature. Not only did he express his high opinion of Robert Bloomfield's *The Farmer's Boy*, but he also, very early, made known its worth to his many friends and it was through him that His Royal Highness, the Duke of York, made a liberal present to the author as an acknowledgement of the pleasure he gained from the perusal of his excellent poem. Sir Charles Bunbury lived at the Hall, burned down in 1914, and here Oliver Goldsmith used to come to stay during his later years. It was his nephew, Sir Henry, who succeeded him, and who was entrusted with the none-too-pleasant task of informing Napoleon Buonaparte of the English Government's determination to banish him to St. Helena.

†The manuscript of *The Farmer's Boy* was bought at a sale of the poet's effects at Shefford in 1824 by a Mr. Baldwin for £14. It is now in the Houghton Library of Harvard University, Massachusetts, U.S.A.

reduce themselves almost wholly to a circumstance of provincial usage, which even well-educated persons in Suffolk and Norfolk do not wholly avoid; and which may be said, as to general custom, to have become in these counties almost an established dialect—that of adopting the plural for singular terminations of verbs, so as to exclude the 'S'. But not a line is added or substantially altered through the whole poem. The proofs have gone through my hands. It has been printed slowly, because most carefully, as it deserved to be printed. I have no doubt of its reception with the public; nor have I any of its going down to posterity with honour, which is not always the fate of productions which are popular in their day. Such indeed are the merits of this work that in true pastoral imagery and simplicity I do not think any production can be put in competition with it since the days of Theocritus.''*

Bloomfield was far from well when the first edition was being prepared by the printers, Messrs Bentley of Bolt Court, Fleet Street, and his brother Nathaniel was first to inform him that he had seen copies of it in a bookshop window in London. Almost at the same time he had been asked by Mr. Lofft to call at the Duke of Grafton's London house in Piccadilly. Much against his will, and under great pressure, for he was very shy and retiring, he went. There he was introduced by Mr. Lofft to the Duke who showed him a large copy of *The Farmer's Boy* beautifully illustrated by Nesbitt, a pupil of the celebrated Bewick of Newcastle-on-Tyne. And the title page bore the motto ''A Shepherd's Boy, he seeks no better name.'' Bloomfield was overcome with emotion. As he left, the Duke pressed into his hand, screwed up in a piece of paper, five guineas. The very next day he sent a copy to his mother at Honington and upon the flyleaf he wrote these words—

> ''To peace and virtue still be true,
> An anxious Mother ever cries,
> Who needs no present to renew
> Parental love—which never dies.
> Yet, when to know, and see and hear
> All that the Great and Good have done,
> This present will be doubly dear
>   Your favour'd poet is—My Son.''

---

*Theocritus. Greek pastoral poet probably a native of Syracuse in Sicily, 310 to 265 B.C. or later. Poet Laureate at the court of Ptolemy II and was the father of bucolic poetry. His characters were real rustics and country scenes are true to life.

So the first edition was at last in print! So well was it received that it sold out within two or three weeks. It is thought that no one poem had ever before attracted so much attention or sold so rapidly. Most of the great people of the land, including many of the most famous writers of the time, showered presents and praise upon the author. The Duke of York sent him 15 guineas and at Hadleigh a local subscription of 12 guineas was raised, the names of the subscribers being given as Thomas Sherlocke Gooch Esq., Major Pocklington, Dr. Gibbons M.D., The Rev. J. Plampin, The Rev. T. Knottesford, The Rev. B. Pritchett, Abram Reeve Esq., Geo. Archer Esq., J. Mills Esq., Mrs. Trail, Mrs. Leake, Nathan Drake, M.D. His financial circumstances improved tremendously and the royalties he received in 1800 alone amounted to £621 - 9 - 0—a vast sum in those days with a purchasing power of about £15,000 today. He was therefore able to move into a self-contained house in The Shepherdess Walk in City Road, a building which was afterwards converted into *The Eagle Tavern*.

Of this his brother George wrote "The only luxury I ever knew him indulge in was a Cockney garden; and here he was more to be pitied than blamed. He staid some time after he came into money in his old lodgings in Mulberry-court, till he was literally hunted out of it. Persons of consideration, who came in great numbers to see him, complained of the place being disagreeable." Mr. Peter George the printer called on him, gave him half a guinea and advised him to get a better situation. Robert then hired a respectable lodging in Short Street, Moorfields. His landlord put the key under the door in the night, and left Robert to pay £9 rent to the proprietor of the house or lose his goods. He then hired a very small house, *The Shepherd and Shepherdess* in the City Road, and there he had what was certainly a large Cockney garden!

About two months later he made his first visit to Honington for twelve years although he had often wished to return. It was spring and the delight he enjoyed is recorded in the lines written at that time—

On revisiting the place of my nativity

"Though Winter's frown had damped the beaming eye,
Through twelve successive Summers heav'd the sigh,
The unaccomplish'd wish was still the same;
Till May in new and sudden glories came!
My heart was rous'd; and Fancy on the wing,
Thus heard the language of enchanting Spring;—

"Come to thy native groves and fruitful fields!
Thou know'st the fragrance that the wild flower yields;
Inhale the breeze that bends the purple bud
And plays along the margin of the wood.
I've cloth'd them all; the very woods where thou
In infancy learn'd'st praise from every bough.
. . . .
O Memory! Shield me from the world's poor strife;
And give these scenes thine everlasting life!"

He records taking his wife and Hannah to see the great oak in Euston Park.

"Myself, my wife and my daughter, Hannah, then nine and a half years old, embraced his rough rind at arm's length, touching our fingers; and could thus encompass it all but about half a yard. By observation afterwards, I found the girth of this tree to be fifteen feet in May 1801."

It was at this time that he and Mr. Capel Lofft got to know each other so well. The admiration of the barrister for his peasant protegé knew no limits, and it was by his efforts and his persistent praise that the influential and literary-minded people of the time were made aware of the worth of Bloomfield's poetry. In his preface to the seventh edition of *The Farmer's Boy* he writes: "I rejoice that I at length have been made personally acquainted with him: that I have seen him here*, and at his mother's and at Bury: that I have discoursed with him: that we have made our rural walks together: that I have heard him read some of those poems which are not yet printed, but which when they shall be, will support fully and extend the fame he has acquired. Though I have spent, occasionally, much of my life among persons worthy of admiration and esteem, I can recollect few days so interesting and so valuable to me as these."

There were times when Mr. Lofft appeared to be rather eccentric, or certainly somewhat unusual, in his reactions. During the first burst of his friendship with Robert Bloomfield he invited him to plant two horse chestnut trees and two oaks in the grounds of his home at Troston Hall. They were given classical names, Homer, Demosthenes, Virgil and Theocritus.

And what of this poem upon which his reputation so securely rests? This wonderful pastoral poem, though one of the simplest in diction, is yet fascinating, entertaining, powerful in description,

---

*Troston.

accurate in every detail, and perhaps one of the finest of its kind in our English language. It has the hallmark of genius stamped unmistakably upon it and it is difficult to understand why, with its great rural appeal and its unparalleled native beauty, it is not better known and more widely read in our own time. It recounts Bloomfield's impressions indelibly fixed in his mind in youth when, as a boy, he lived and worked so close to nature. In it he traces the farmer's boy, Giles he calls him, through the four seasons of the year, and in so doing describes, in his own inimitable way, the situations he meets in the rural world, of his day and age, on the farm and in the countryside which he knew so well. Giles is a veritable cavalier of the Suffolk countryside.

> "Strange to the world, he wore a bashful look.
> The fields his study, Nature was his book."

To be appreciated and enjoyed the whole poem must be read in its entirety. It contains but some 1500 lines and is crammed full of the best imagery and polished versification. While Jane Austen was describing life as it was for the upper middle classes in her *Pride and Prejudice* and other novels, Bloomfield was telling the world what it was like for the humble poor. Very near the beginning of the poem he wrote:

> "Live, trifling incidents, and grace my song,
> That to the humblest menial belong."

Of Giles he says—

> "No stripes, no tyranny his steps pursued;
> His life was cheerful, constant servitude."

The scene is then laid for all that follows:—

> "Where noble Grafton spreads his rich domains,
> Round Euston's watered vale, and sloping plains,
> Where woods and groves in solemn grandeur rise,
> Where the kite brooding unmolested flies;
> The wood cock and the painted pheasant race,
> And skulking foxes, destined for the chase;
> There Giles, untaught and unrepining stray'd
> Through every copse, and grove, and winding glade;
> There his first thought to Nature's charms inclined,
> That stamps devotion on th'enquiring mind.
> A little farm his generous master till'd,

Who with peculiar grace his station fill'd;
By deeds of hospitality endear'd,
Serv'd from affection, for his worth rever'd;
A happy offspring blest his plenteous board,
His fields were fruitful, and his barns well stor'd,
And fourscore ewes he fed; a sturdy team;
And lowing kine that graz'd beside the stream:
Unceasing industry he kept in view;
And never lack'd a job for Giles to do."

He describes the lambs in Spring scurrying over the fields—

"Away they scour, impetuous, ardent, strong,
The green turf trembling as they bound along."

And when the butcher comes to take them away—

"Ah! fallen rose! sad emblem of their doom;
Frail as thyself, they perish as they bloom."

In Summer, the farmer, always anxious about the crops and the weather—

"But views the future with the present hours,
And looks for failures as he looks for showers."

Watching the skylark flying off into the distance Giles notes that—

"The flutt'ring songstress a mere speck became,
Like fancy's floating bubbles in a dream."

Here is an example of the pronunciation of words as they were spoken in the very late eighteenth century. Dream is pronounced 'drame' to rhyme with came. There are numerous other instances in Bloomfield for he rarely makes a faulty rhyme.

Now for the beginning of harvest—

"Here, midst the boldest triumphs of her worth,
Nature herself invites the reapers forth;
Dares the keen sickle from its twelvemonth's rest,
And gives that ardour which in every breast
From Infancy to Age alike appears,
When the first sheaf its plumy top uprears."

And regarding the reapers themselves—

"Summer's light garb itself now cumbrous grown,
Each his thin doublet in the shade throws down;
Where oft the mastiff skulks with half-shut eye,
And rouses at the stranger passing by."

Then the dairymaid arrives upon the scene to watch the men at work—

> "For, lo, encircled there, the lovely Maid,
> In youth's own bloom and native smiles array'd;
> Her hat awry, divested of her gown,
> Her creaking stays of leather, stout and brown;—
> Invidious barrier! Why art thou so high,
> When the slight covering of her neck slips by,
> There half-revealing to the eager sight,
> Her full, ripe bosom, exquisitely white?
> In many a local tale of harmless mirth,
> And many a jest of momentary birth,
> She bears a part, and as she stops to speak,
> Strokes back the ringlets from her glowing cheek."

So the plot unfolds until, at the end of harvest, in the old farm-house—

> "Behold the sound oak table's massy frame
> Bestride the kitchen floor! the careful dame
> And gen'rous host invite their friends around,
> For all that clear'd the crop or till'd the ground,
> Are guests by right of custom:— old and young;
> And many a neighbouring yeoman join the throng,
> With artisans that lent their dex'trous aid,
> When o'er each field the flaming sunbeams play'd."

> . . . .

> "Here once a year Distinction low'rs its crest.
> The master, servant, and the merry guest,
> Are equal all; and round the happy ring
> The reaper's eyes exulting glances fling,
> And warmed with gratitude, he quits his place,
> With sunburnt hands and ale-enlivened face,
> Refills the jug his honoured host to tend,
> To serve at once the master and the friend;
> Proud, thus, to meet his smiles, to share his tale,
> His nuts, his conversation and his ale."

In Autumn he tells of the church and the churchyard and also of some of those who congregate there—

> "Mean structure, where no bones of heroes lie!
> The rude inelegance of poverty

Reign here alone: else why that roof of straw?
These narrow windows with the frequent flaw?
O'er whose low cells the dock and mallow spread,
And rampant nettles lift the spiry head,
Whilst from the hollows of the tower on high
The grey capp'd daws in saucy legions fly.
Round these lone walls assembling neighbours meet
And tread departed friends beneath their feet;
And new-briar'd graves, that prompt the secret sigh,
Shew each the spot where he himself must lie.

. . . .

Hither at times, with cheerfulness of soul,
Sweet village maids from neighbouring hamlets stroll,
That like the light-heeled does, o'er lawns that rove,
Look shyly curious; ripening into love;
For love's their errand."

Perhaps one of the most exciting of all his accounts of rural pursuits is his saga of fox-hunting in the eighteenth century. The scene is laid, of course, in that tiny piece of England which was so dear to his heart, and about which he so frequently writes. It is—

"Where smiling Euston boasts her good Fitzroy,
Lord of pure alms, and gifts that wide extend;
The farmer's patron and the poor man's friend:"

Some eighty-two lines are devoted to the subject culminating in the death of Trouncer, one of the best and most trusty hounds of the Euston pack. There is never any indication that Bloomfield regards the sport as cruel and Bloomfield was a gentle, kindly man. Rather does he rejoice with the countryman of his own day in the thrills of the chase through his own inimitable Giles, whom as the "Crusoe of the lonely fields" comes forth from the improvised bird-watcher's hut in the Park to regret the passing of the summer, yet at the same time to "welcome the new harmony which pervades the solemn wood". This is great music, this unparalleled verse. Giles is in ecstasy here telling of the baying of the hounds bursting forth "mad with joy" from their kennels to chase the fox across the slopes and lawns of the Park and through all its coverts and the forest glades. The huntsman's mellow horn, the view halloo, the joyous cries of the hounds and the shouts of the following villagers all mingle to provide a rustic rhapsody.

Then comes silence, faltering silence, for a while, till the leading hound, Trouncer, sounds the note that calls them all to action once again. And so the hunt goes on o'er hill and dale and dashing stream, across the fens and meadows and back again beneath the enormous oak trees of the Park until the stiff-limbed peasants can go no further and have to give up the pursuit.

But Trouncer is ageing too and Trouncer dies:

> "Poor faithful Trouncer! thou canst lead no more;
> All thy fatigues and all thy triumphs o'er!
> . . . .
> Pride of thy race! with worth far less than thine,
> Full many human leaders daily shine!
> . . . .
> Each sportsman heard the tidings with a sigh,
> When Death's cold touch had stopt his tuneful cry;
> And though high deeds, and fair exalted praise,
> In memory liv'd and flow'd in rustic lays,
> Short was the strain of monumental woe:
> Foxes rejoice! here buried lies your foe."

But Trouncer has gone down to posterity quite outside the ambit of the poem for the then Duke of Grafton had him buried by the wall of Euston Hall, and upon a stone in the wall itself was recorded simply this:

TROUNCER
1788
Foxes rejoice
Here buried lies your Foe.

We know that Robert Bloomfield came home to Honington to visit his mother in 1788, and there can be no doubt whatsoever that he saw this stone in Euston Park and read its inscription, since the identical words appear in *The Farmer's Boy*. It is possible that he was present at its erection or even at the actual interment; for the burial of a hound such as Trouncer would have merited the same solemnity as would the burial of any other faithful servant of the aristocracy of that time. The stone would most likely have been put in position immediately after the burial.

So to Winter where he elaborates upon the anxieties of the farmer and his men during winter; the care of the cattle and the horses, and the watching of the lambs and the sheep—until Giles having worked conscientiously throughout the year, joyfully anticipates another spring.

"Another spring!" his heart exulting cries;
"Another year! with promised blessings rise!
Eternal Power! from whom these blessings flow,
Teach me still more to wonder, more to know:
Seed-time and Harvest let me see again;
Wander the leaf-strewn wood, the frozen plain:
Let the first flower, corn-waving field, plain, tree,
Here round my home, still lift my soul to thee;
And let me ever, midst thy bounties, raise
An humble note of thankfulness and praise."

Here we detect his joy, through Giles, at the contemplated return of Spring, and the hope that the new year will bring him "blessings" as he calls them. There is also an underlying longing for a return to his native place, which he had not seen, at that time, for at least ten years.

The poem was later translated into French, Italian and Latin, and, in more recent years, it has been put into Japanese. Here are Bloomfield's whimsical observations to the Rev. W. Clubbe of Brandeston in Suffolk, who translated it into Latin under the title *Agricola Puer*, *Poema Robertii Bloomfield Celiberrimum*:

"Hey, Giles! in what new garb art drest?
For lads like you methinks a bold one;
I'm glad to see thee so carest;
But hark ye! don't despise your old one.
Thou'rt not the first by many a Boy
Who've found abroad good friends to own 'em;
Then, in such coats, have shown their joy
E'en their own fathers have not known 'em."

In 1801 an edition was published in Philadelphia U.S.A. by James Humphreys, and reprints were made of *The Farmer's Boy* and other poems in succeeding years at New York, Baltimore and Philadelphia, so that Bloomfield's sister, Elizabeth, was able to write to him in 1805 from America saying, "Your poems make a great bustle here. Before I left Philadelphia, the Governor of the State of Jersey sent for me. He is an original in his manner: his name is Bloomfield, and every one of that name he meets with he sends for, and examines his genealogy to find if they spring from the same branch. I assure you I have not been so catechized since I was a baby: he seemed to wish to find himself allied to the poet as he was pleased to call you. He is an old man; he tells me his great-great-grandfather fled from England, in the time of the revolution in England, in the time of Cromwell.

This letter was dated February 11th 1805 and came from George Town, Potomac, where Elizabeth then resided, and where she had founded a fashionable milliner's establishment.

Robert Bloomfield's house in the City Road was not large, but it was sufficient for his family; then himself, his wife, three daughters and a son. In it he was able to live fairly comfortably and somewhat in keeping with his new-found station in life. How appropriately was it named *The Shepherd and Shepherdess*. He was able also to buy good books and pictures and some very fine mahogany furniture, and one of Hawkins' patent writing machines.* He was already well-informed in literary matters, having read many of the works of Shakespeare, Spencer, Dryden and the great Samuel Johnson to name but a few. It is safe to say that he had read very widely in all the fields of English literature and we find him observing in one of his many letters to his brother George: "I have read Gay's *Trivia;* it descends to minute descriptions of London, more minute than mine do of the country," and of Johnson: "I always look at him and his abilities with a mixture of reverence and anger." Here he was able to receive many callers from all walks of life—artists, actors, poets, clergymen as well as men and women of the fashionable and business world, and from here he began to receive invitations to visit many rich and distinguished people in their own homes. He was much sought after and became tremendously popular. There is no doubt that he was a most likeable man. The highest in the land paid court to him, and he became their guest. On many occasions the Duke of Grafton welcomed him at his Piccadilly house, where he saw again, amongst other celebrities, the Prince Regent and Beau Brummel and, no doubt the actress Mrs. Siddons as well as the poetess, Mrs. Anna Laetitia Barbauld, and Mrs. Elizabeth Inchbald, the actress-daughter of a Stanningfield, Suffolk, farmer. The Prince entertained him several times at Carlton House, where he met Mrs. Fitzherbert, the Prince's companion until 1803. Bloomfield would sometimes give a demonstration of his prodigious memory to those present: it was the Duke who liked to show off his prodigy to his friends, and it is said he would give him a book of poems which he had never seen before, and Bloomfield, after reading only once over some four or five hundred lines, would repeat them verbatim without a mistake. His memory was truly astonishing. He could repeat with verbal accuracy *The Seasons*, *The Castle of Indolence*, and nearly all Burns' poems. He was unable to account for his power of memory, and used to assert that

---

*An early typewriter.

it was a subject on which he had never bestowed any attention. It appeared strange to him that other men's memories should be weaker than his own, and he regarded his gift with indifference. Among the people he got to know at this time were Samuel Rogers, the banker poet, who was famous for his breakfast parties, his brother Henry Rogers, and Edward Jenner the discoverer of the vaccine against smallpox. All these remained his life-long friends. Another man who figured greatly in his life at that time was the Earl of Buchan, who frequently sought his company and pressed him to visit him in Scotland at Dryburgh Abbey. Despite his tremendous admiration for Burns and his expressed desire to see the Caledonian hills he refused, saying "I have ardent wishes on that point and have some reasons, which rise up against their completion, two of which are Burns is dead— or I might have seen him and I am married." He did, however, make a beautiful pair of shoes for the Earl's wife and sent them to her in Edinburgh with a poem entitled *Emma's Kid*.

Regarding Burns, he wrote later—

"Miss Johnson, with whom I dined at the White Hart Inn, Fetter Lane, was personally acquainted with Burns; who, breakfasting with her, drank a large tumbler previous to taking either eatables or tea, saying that he had been up till three in the morning, and had drunk too much wine. On Miss J's remonstrating with him as to the injury to which he exposed his health, he replied, 'Madam, they would not thank me for my company, if I did not drink with them, I must give them a slice of my constitution.' I wish Burns had given them thinner slices of his constitution, that it might have lasted longer; I then might possibly have had the pleasure of seeing him. He died but two months after I began composing *The Farmer's Boy* though at that time, and long after, his death and history were unknown to me."

Bloomfield was ever conscious of the debt he owed to his mother in that she gave him such a happy and memorable childhood, and now that he was able to repay her in some measure he did so by taking her to stay with him in his new home for several months, in fact until the Suffolk countryside called her back home. But her son was far from well. Despite his success and the adulation he received from his admirers, he still had not infrequent bouts of melancholia, and was troubled too with rheumatism and very bad headaches. But when he felt at all fit he liked to read and to sketch. He was no mean artist for some of his work at this time has been preserved. Among other sketches was one of his own garden, and another of his home in Honington. After all was he not descended, on the maternal side, from the great Sir Godfrey Kneller (1648 - 1723), the famous portrait-painter of German birth who was knighted by William III and made a baronet by George I? He took regular walks out into the Moorfields and his neighbours knew him as a 'slender dark little man, hardly more than five feet tall of melancholy appearance whose goodness of disposition and mildness of temper were the subject of much comment.'

He wrote and perfected a great deal of poetry during his first two years in the City Road, and in 1802 his second volume of poems was published. It was called *Rural Tales, Ballads and Songs*. This work greatly enhanced his reputation. He loved the country and he loved its people and it was of them that his sweetest songs were sung. Amongst these ballads, for ballads they mostly were, came the Suffolk Fair-Day Ballad *Richard and Kate*, in which Bloomfield probably had his own experiences at Bardwell Fair in mind, *The Miller's Maid,* * *Walter and Jane* and the popular local tale, *The Fakenham Ghost*. This last has stood the test of time and has been remembered and frequently recited in the district of its origin ever since it was written.

This compelling and intriguing ballad is of no mean order. It captures the superstitious atmosphere of the period and is founded upon fact. When the incident occurred is uncertain, but Bloomfield suggests that it might well have taken place in the early 1700's, very soon after the Fitzroys had established themselves at Euston. He said in 1802, "The circumstance occurred, perhaps, long before I was born; but is still related by my mother and some of the oldest inhabitants in that part of the country."

It tells, in the skilful manner in which all these rural tales are told, how an elderly house-servant of the Graftons was making her way home, after nightfall, from the Hall at Euston across the Park to her home in Park Cottages at Little Fakenham. It is still possible for anyone wishing to recapture the eerie sensation of the walk to trace the route she followed on that fateful night by way of the Temple and the boundary wall down the old drive to the Hall, across to the hawthorn ride and through the large white gate to the cottages by Mickle Hill.

As she hurried along, her footsteps disturbed the rooks in the trees of the copse she must pass by, and the sheep sheltering below scurried away. Then she heard quick short steps behind her, but when she stopped to investigate, the steps ceased. She tried to run away but the steps followed her. She stopped again and peered through the

---

The Miller's Maid. In 1968 a Mr. J. H. Cooke of Santa Fé, New Mexico, U.S.A. called on the authors at Honington and said that he remembered learning the whole of *The Miller's Maid* at school, as a boy, in New Mexico.

darkness only to descry a grey monster in the distance. Panic-stricken now, she knelt down, confessed her sins and prayed, but still the "ghost" came on. At last she reached the white gate, and, pushing it so hard in her terror, she made it swing long enough to allow the "ghost" to follow her through. She fainted. Outside her cottage door her husband and daughter awaited her return. By the light of a candle they saw, not far away, an ass's foal which had lost its way in the Park and had strayed from its mother. This was the "ghost" which had terrified the woman. They took it in to their home and kept it as a pet, its very existence helping to belie, perhaps, many of the goblin tales so rife in Suffolk in those far-off days.

Here it is interesting to note an observation made by Bloomfield in after years:

"While my *Rural Tales* were printing, I first got sight of Mr. Wordsworth's Ballads and was startled to find him saying in *The Idiot Boy*—

'That Pony's worth his weight in gold.'

I had written, without seeing or dreaming of Mr. Wordsworth's remarks, almost the same words in *Market Night*.

'That Beast is worth his weight in gold.'

Now if unborn critics should dispute about this, as I fear they will about many such trifles, I would say, could I rise from the grave, 'Mr. W. wrote and published his book first, and I had not seen it. I would beg the learned searchers after imitations and curious co-incidences, to give all reasonable scope to charity, and to admit, in all cases, the kindred ideas which must exist in tracing the same subject'."

Bloomfield was again much sought after socially as a result of his second volume of poems. Appreciation of the work came from all quarters, and the books sold like wildfire. Two famous people came into his life at this time. They were the Rt. Hon. C. J. Fox, one of George III's most able Ministers, whom Burke described as one of the greatest debaters the world had ever seen, and, again, the Earl of Buchan, both of whom admired his work and sought his company.

Mr. Fox was tremendously impressed by *The Miller's Maid* and found time, busy as he was with matters of state, to write several times to Bloomfield. The Earl of Buchan's favourite poem was *Richard and Kate*, and we know that Bloomfield recited it at least three times to the Earl and his lady. Buchan persuaded him to attend celebrations of peace with France, at Ranelagh in May 1802. His wife Mary Anne rarely went far from home but on this occasion she accompanied him to witness the great display of fireworks that took place there on that occasion and they did not return home until morning. He has recorded his great joy and excitement in his poem *A Visit to Ranelagh*, as well as in a letter to the Earl in which he also mentions that he has lately dined with Mrs. Barbauld, the poetess. Another of his friends at this period was George Dyer* who was also a friend of Lamb. This is very strange since Charles Lamb was one of those who did not appreciate Bloomfield's work and did not hesitate to say so. Writing to Manning in 1800 about *The Farmer's Boy* he said "Don't you think the fellow who wrote it has a poor mind? I have just opened him, but he makes me sick!" But Byron some years later in *English Bards and Scots Reviewers* referred to Bloomfield in most complimentary terms.

Robert Southey, who had already reviewed *The Farmer's Boy* most favourably in *The Critical* again came out loudly in praise of the *Tales*, an American edition of which appeared in Burlington N.J. in 1803. Bloomfield was very happy now and speaks of having two guests, often overlooked, in his house, Health and Happiness.

Among Robert Bloomfield's Suffolk friends and admirers was Dr. Drake of Hadleigh, a noted Shakespearian critic of his day. Both he and Bloomfield became interested in the great Dr. Jenner's discovery of the smallpox vaccine and his experiments in connection with it at the turn of the century. As early as January 1802 we find Robert writing to Drake, sending him a copy of his *Rural Tales* and at the same time thanking him and his wife for their continued hospitality. In the same letter he exclaims: "What think you of the Vaccine? Is it not a glorious cause?" From that moment he occupies his mind with the idea of a poem in praise of Jenner and his work.

Jenner, who was practising in his home town of Berkeley in Gloucestershire had, like many others of standing, his London house, and by July 21st, 1802, Bloomfield is able to write to his brother George to the effect that he has met Jenner, who by that time had become a kind of hero in the mind of the poet. "I have seen Dr. Jenner," he wrote "and his kindness almost induced me to show him the little progress I have made in pursuit of his subject; but I, suddenly determined to the contrary, and doubted of the propriety of so doing." On that same day he was invited to take tea at Jenner's house. Their friendship developed and with it grew Bloomfield's anxiety to produce a poem through which he could help to popularise the Doctor's all-important vaccine.

In March 1803 Jenner was in London, and he again contacted Bloomfield. On May 17th we find him as a guest at the Doctor's

*George Dyer, 1755-1841, English scholar and historian.

53rd birthday party singing a song of his own composition, in honour of the occasion. There were six verses in all but the last two mentioned Jenner specifically by name:

"All nations shall feel, and all nations inherit
The wonderful blessing we place in their view;
And if in that blessing a mortal claims merit,
Oh! Jenner—your country resigns it to you!

From the field, from the farm, comes the glorious treasure,
May its life-saving impulse—all fresh as the morn—
Still spread round the earth, without bounds, without measure,
Till Time has forgot when his Jenner was born."

Appropriately enough it was on May 17th the next year (1804), that his *Good Tidings or News From The Farm* was published. This poem was well received and was popular, chiefly because the subject with which it dealt had captured the interest of almost everyone. Several titles had been suggested for it by Capel Loffts and by Jenner himself, but "The Vaccine Rose" and "Vaccine Innoculation" did not appeal to Bloomfield, who could only link it with his early life, with his own father's death, with the cow and with the farm. In his Advertisement to the poem he refers to the horrors of the smallpox as he saw it in his childhood, "The account given of my infancy and of my father's burial is not only poetically but strictly true, and with me it has its weight accordingly. I have witnessed the destruction described in my brother's family; and I have, in my own, insured by vaccine innoculation, the lives of four children, who I trust are destined to look back upon the small-pox as the scourge of days gone by." It was recited on the day of its publication at a special meeting of The Royal Jennerian Society in London. Jenner himself was present and was so pleased with its sentiment and its reception and by the fact that he was mentioned by name in it, that he presented the author with a very fine inkstand, which Bloomfield treasured to the end of his life.

Later, in one of his popular songs, *Irish News*, Bloomfield again writes about the smallpox pimple and the vaccine obtained from the cow.

During his journey down the Wye in 1807 he found time to call on Jenner, who was then at Cheltenham, and sent a gift, a silver tea caddy, home to Bloomfield's wife, Mary Anne. This tea-caddy was sold at the sale of Bloomfield's effects in 1824.

It is strange to note that both Bloomfield and Jenner died in the same year 1823, Jenner being then 72 and Bloomfield 56.

The Duke of Grafton, ever anxious for Bloomfield's welfare, felt that he should be given some congenial work in a government office. Accordingly he found him a post as under-sealer in the Seal Office at Somerset House. Here he was to act as assistant to a Captain Allen the Master Sealer, to whose office it was intended he should ultimately succeed. The salary of the Master was very high and was made up of a fixed salary, fees and fines. In particular it was his privilege to impose a fine of sixpence on each deed sealed after 4 p.m., a privilege which he liked so well that it was his custom to set the office clock on about ten minutes every afternoon. This villainy occasioned constant disputes with the lawyers and their clerks, who objected to being so transparently defrauded. To render Bloomfield's discomfort more intense, Captain Allen used to appeal to him to confirm his lies. He tolerated this misery for only a few weeks, and one day unceremoniously quitted the Seal Office while a veritable riot was in progress there.

3   His Love Poems

Although Robert Bloomfield was not the great lover that Burns was, he was certainly not the dull unemotional philanthropist that some would have us believe, obsessed only with the beauty of the Suffolk countryside and steeped in the folklore of its people. He knew and had experienced the joys and the pangs of love, that is the love of a man for a woman. And the poems which he has written leave us in no doubt about this, for they contain much of the sentiment of Burns and the intensity of Byron, and their unaffected simplicity gives them freshness and sincerity. *Nancy* in particular is certainly to be placed amongst the gems of love songs, especially since it was written to his very first love. In this poem he refers to "the grove", evidently Lanket's Grove mentioned elsewhere in this book.

NANCY

"You ask me, dear Nancy, what makes me presume
That you cherish a secret affection for me?
When we see the flowers bud, don't we look for the bloom?
Then, sweetest, attend while I answer to thee.

When we young men with pastimes the twilight beguile,
I watch your plump cheek till it dimples with joy;
And observe, that whatever occasions the smile,
You give me a glance, but provokingly coy.

Last month, when wild strawberries pluck'd in the grove,
Like beads on the tall seeded grass you had strung;
You gave me the choicest; I hoped 'twas for love:
And I told you my hopes while the nightingale sung.

Remember the viper—'twas close at your feet,
How you started and threw yourself into my arms;
Not a strawberry there was so ripe nor so sweet
As the lips which I kissed to subdue your alarms.

As I pulled down the clusters of nuts for my Fair
What a blow I received from a strong bending bough;
Though Lucy and other gay lasses were there,
Not one of them showed such compassion as you.

And was it compassion?—by Heaven 'twas more!
A telltale betrays you;—that blush on your cheek.
Then come, dearest Maid, all your trifling give o'er,
And whisper what Candour will teach you to speak."

But Bloomfield is not confined to the adoration of one woman.
Throughout his works we find him ever ready to extol the virtues and
attractions of the female. A delightful little song of just two verses is
found in his drama *Hazelwood Hall*. It is sung by young Joel, a wheelwright in the play, who is deeply in love with Mary Maythorn,
"Mary up at the Hall".

THE GIRL OF MY HEART

"Then why should the girl of my heart
For whom all these raptures I feel,
Be rivall'd by wagon or cart,
And slip through my hands like an eel?

I am young—so is she—and how fair!
Then love shall my moments employ;
I am caught by her berry-brown hair,
And the rose on her cheek is my joy."

The mill, in the following verses addressed to Lucy, is certainly
Sapiston Mill, a watermill still in use. The meadowsweet still grows
in profusion by the stream, the Blackbourne, and the maybush or

hawthorn is more abundant here than anywhere else in Suffolk. To Lucy, then, he offers all the beauty of the countryside in May. What ecstasy!

LUCY: A SONG

"Thy favourite bird is soaring still:
My Lucy haste thee oe'r the dale;
The stream's let loose, and from the mill
All silent comes the balmy gale:
  Yet so lightly on its way,
  Seems to whisper, 'Holiday'

The pathway flowers that bending meet
And give the meads their yellow hue,
The May-bush and the meadow-sweet
Reserve their fragrance all for you.
  Why then, Lucy, why delay?
  Let us share the holiday.

Since there thy smiles, my charming maid,
Are with unfeigned rapture seen,
To beauty be the homage paid;
Come, claim the triumph of the green.
  Here's my hand, come, come away;
  Share the merry holiday.

A promise to my Lucy made
(And shall my heart its claim resign?)
That ere May-flowers again should fade,
Her heart and hand should both be mine.
  Hark ye, Lucy, this is May;
  Love shall crown our holiday."

In September 1804 he visited the Whittlebury Forest in Northamptonshire, and it was from here that he wrote some wonderful lines to his wife; and this after more than fourteen years of marriage—a marriage which had been fraught with poverty, sickness and disappointment.

TO MARY

"I rise, dear Mary, from the soundest rest,
A wandering, wayworn, musing, singing guest.
I claim the privilege of hill and plain;
Mine are the weeds and all that they contain;
The unpolluted gale which sweeps the glade;
All the cool blessings of the solemn shade;
Health and the flow of happiness sincere;
Yet there's one wish,—I wish that thou wert here;
Free from the trammels of domestic care,
With me these dear autumnal sweets to share;
To share my heart's ungovernable joy;
And keep the birthday of our poor lame boy.
Ah! that's the tender string! Yet since I find
That scenes like these can soothe the harrass'd mind,
Trust me, 'twould set thy jaded spirits free,
To wander thus through vales and woods with me.
Thou know'st how much I love to steal away
From noise, from uproar and the blaze of day;
With double transport would my heart rebound
To lead where the clustering nuts are found;
No toilsome efforts would our task demand,
For the brown treasure stoops to meet the hand.
Round the tall hazel, beds of moss appear
In green swards nibbled by the forest deer.
Sun and alternate shade; while o'er our heads
The cawing rook his glossy pinions spreads;
The noisy jay, his wild woods dashing through;
The ring-dove's chorus, and the rustling bough;
The far resounding gate; the kite's shrill scream;
The distant ploughman's halloo to his team.
This is the chorus to my soul so dear;
It would delight thee, too, wert thou but here:
For we might talk of home and muse o'er days
Of sad distress, and Heaven's mysterious ways;
Our chequered fortunes, with a smile retrace,
And build new hopes upon our infant race;
Pour our thanksgivings forth, and weep the while;
Or pray for blessings on our native isle.
But vain the wish! Mary thy sighs forbear,
Nor grudge the pleasure which thou canst not share;
Make home delightful, kindly wish for me,
And I'll leave hills, and dales, and woods for thee."

40

Here, as in so many of his poems, he allies himself and his absorbing love of the countryside with his love for womankind. To him they are one and the same emotion, a dangerous supposition, and the woman he loves must love the natural world which he loves and share with him his enjoyment of it. In return she merits his unqualified loyalty. He also expects his woman to believe that it is only the love of the beauty and wonder of nature that can ever keep him from her side. And in his *Mary's Evening Sigh* he makes Mary express his own very thoughts in the final verse of the poem. Her lover comes not home, and she awaits his coming with the calm assurance that he stays not with another, but that only the woodland charms detain him.

"Thou art not false! that cannot be;
Yet I my rivals deem
Each woodland charm, the moss, the tree,
The silence and the stream:
Whate'er my love, detains thee now,
I'll yet forgive thy stay;
But with tomorrow's dawn come thou.
We'll brush the dews away."

The Woodland Hallo, *The Maid of Dunstable*, *The Soldier's Return*, *The Man in the Moon* and *Kentish Mary* all speak of love. His affection for Rosy Hannah was strong enough to follow him into marriage and his eldest daughter was named Hannah after her, but who she was remains a mystery.

Not only was he able to feel a man's emotional unbalance, but he could put himself in the woman's place as well, as we have seen above. But it is in the *Gleaner's Song*, written during his journey down the Wye, that he excels. In this unique poetical effusion he gives us something which few poets have ever achieved in such entirety, and at the same time in the beauty of simplicity. Here, then, is the pre-marital song of a simple and virtuous country maiden.

GLEANER'S SONG

"Dear Ellen, your tales are all plenteously stored
With the joys of some bride, and the wealth of her lord:
    Of her chariots and dresses,
    And worldly caresses,
And servants that fly when she's waited upon:
But what can she boast if she weds unbeloved?
Can she e'er feel the joy that one morning I proved,
When I put on my new-gown and waited for John.

These fields, my dear Ellen, I knew them of yore,
Yet to me they ne'er looked so enchanting before;
      The distant bells ringing,
      The birds round us singing,
For pleasure is pure when affection is won;
They told me the troubles and cares of a wife;
But I loved him, and that was the pride of my life
When I put on my new-gown and waited for John.

He shouted and ran, as he leapt from the stile;
And what in my bosom was passing the while?
      For love knows the blessing
      Of ardent caressing,
When virtue inspires us and doubts are all gone.
The sunshine of Fortune you say is divine;
True love and the sunshine of Nature were mine,
When I put on my new-gown and waited for John.''

4   The Sea and the River Wye

In 1804 Bloomfield's mother became seriously ill at Honington and he took coach home to the village to be with her, and stayed until her death on December 27th. She was buried in Honington Churchyard beside her first husband on December 31st and a stone to mark her tomb was given by the Duke of Grafton. The following inscription was carved upon it, but it is, alas, no longer legible.

Beneath this stone are deposited the mortal remains of Elizabeth Glover, who died December 1804. Her maiden name was Manby, and she was twice married: By her first husband, who lies buried near this spot, she was the mother of six children, the youngest of whom was Robert Bloomfield, the Pastoral Poet. In her household affairs she was a pattern of industry, cleanliness, and every domestic virtue. By her kind, her meek, and inoffensive behaviour, she had conciliated the sincere good-will of all her neighbours and acquaintances. Nor amid the busy cares of time was she ever forgetful of eternity. But her religion was no hypocritical service, no vain form of words!!!—It consisted in loving God and keeping his commandments as they have been made known to us by Jesus Christ.

READER!
Go thou and do likewise.

When the churchyard was levelled in 1963 and many of the grave-stones were removed or placed by the walls, the headstone of Mrs. Glover was left in its original position. There was no stone to mark the grave of her husband, Robert's father, so the footstone from her own grave was placed at the head of his, where it now stands with the initials E.G. carved upon it.

The poet was overcome with grief at the loss of one to whom he owed so much and whose deeply religious attitude to life had influenced his own way of life so greatly at all times. Here is an account of the last stage of her life together with his first almost perfect essay in blank verse, which he addressed to the spindle which she left half-filled when she died.

He tells us that his mother's portrait was taken on her last visit to London in the summer of 1804, and about six months previous to her death. During the period of evident decline in her strength and faculties, she conceived, in place of that patient resignation which she had before felt, an ungovernable dread of ultimate want, and observed to a relative with peculiar emphasis, that 'to meet Winter, Old Age, and Poverty, was like meeting three great giants'. To the last hour of her life she was an excellent spinner; and latterly, the peculiar kind of wool which she spun was brought exclusively for her, as being the one in the village who exercised their industry on so fine a sort. During the tearful paroxysms of her last depression she spun with the utmost violence, and with vehemence exclaimed—'I must spin!' A paralytic affection struck her whole right side while at work, and obliged her to quit her spindle when only half-filled, and she died within a fortnight afterwards. He concludes, "I have that spindle now. She returned from her visit to London on Friday the 29th of June, just, to a day, twenty-three years after she brought me to London, which was also on a Friday, in the year 1781". His address to *The Spindle* shows his mastery of blank verse.

TO A SPINDLE

"Relic! I will not bow to thee nor worship!
Yet, treasure as thou art, remembrancer
Of sunny days, that ever haunt my dreams,
When thy brown fellows as a task I twirled,
And sung my ditties, ere the Farm receiv'd

My vagrant foot, and with its liberty
And all its cheerful buds and opening flowers
Had taught my heart to wander—
              Relic of affection, come;
Thou shalt a moral teach to me and mine,
The hand that wore thee smooth is cold, and spins
No more. Debility press'd hard around
The seat of life, and terrors fill'd her brain;
Nor causeless terrors; Giants grim and bold,
Three Mighty ones she fear'd to meet; they came—
Winter, Old Age, and Poverty, all came:
The last had dropp'd his club, yet fancy made
Him formidable; and when Death beheld
Her tribulation, he fulfilled his task,
And to her trembling hand and heart at once,
Cried, "Spin no more." Thou then wert left half fill'd
With this soft downy fleece, such as she wound
Through all her days! She who could spin so well!
Half-fill'd wert thou, half-finished when she died.
Half finished! 'tis the motto of the world!
We spin vain threads, and dream, and strive and die
With sillier things than spindles in our hands."

This was his last visit to Honington, and although in his latter years
he often yearned for the scenes of his youth he never came back. On
his return to London, after his mother's funeral, he found that both
Mary Anne his wife and his favourite child, the ailing six-year-old,
Charles, had been ill. Upon the moment he decided to send them away
for a holiday—a long holiday by the sea. Medical practitioners of that
time were prescribing sea-air and sea-bathing for certain complaints, so
what could be better for his dear ones than some months by the sea?
Accordingly they were sent to Worthing. The family was well off now
and could well afford a cottage on the fashionable Sussex coast, and
their father was also able to spend some weeks with them later that
summer. It was the year of Trafalgar, 1805, and, strange as it may seem,
although he was now nearly forty years of age, he had never yet seen
the sea. It was on his way across the Sussex Downs to Worthing that
he first caught sight of it, and recorded his excitement in this verse
taken from his poem written on Chankbury Hill—

A FIRST VIEW OF THE SEA

"But what's yon southward dark blue line
Along the horizon's utmost bound;
On which the weary clouds recline,
Still varying half the circle round?
The sea! the sea! My God! the sea!
You sunbeams on its bosom play!
With milkwhite sails expanded free,
There ploughs the bark on her cheerful way!"

It is strange that he never saw the sea, nor the Suffolk coast, from Yarmouth or Lowestoft or Crabbe's Aldeburgh.

In 1806 came his third volume of poems, *Wild Flowers*, dedicated to his son, Charles, in the hope that the income from the sale of it might provide for his needs in the years ahead, for he was lame. *The Mirror* of 1826 has this to say about it—"Of all Bloomfield's published works, no volume has alone so much interest as his *Wild Flowers*." It was a veritable garland of country stories. Of the poems in this collection *The Horkey*, *The Broken Crutch*, *My Old Oak Table* and *Barnham Water* are outstanding. This last was written in the summer of 1802 when the poet was on his way from Honington, via Euston Hall and the Blackbourne streamlet to Thetford to visit his sister Catherine who lived there. It is a charming, if somewhat sentimental piece of local loveliness.

The Horkey is a tale in the Suffolk dialect, and Bloomfield in his own peculiar way makes it to be told by one of the 'characters' of the village, a certain Judie Twitchet, who knits as she talks and describes the fun and the feasting which takes place in a Honington farmhouse after the harvest, and stops only when her ball of worsted has 'run out'.

In creating this situation Bloomfield has become, perhaps, more Chaucerian than Chaucer himself, for Judie Twitchett, he tells us, was a real person. She had lived with his mother's cousin, a Mrs. Bannock of Honington, and died long before the poem was written. It became necessary, therefore for him to "resurrect" her in order to enable her to tell the story, which describes a harvest-home feast of the middle of the eighteenth century.

In his "Advertisement" which precedes the poem he has this to say, by way of explanation.

"In the descriptive ballad which follows, it will be evident that I have endeavoured to preserve the style of a gossip, and to transmit the memorial of a custom, the extent or antiquity of which I am not acquainted with, and pretend not to inquire. In Suffolk husbandry, the man who, whether by merit or sufferance I know not, goes foremost through the harvest with the scythe or the sickle, is honoured with the title of "Lord", and at the Horkey or harvest-home feast, collects what he can, for himself and brethren, from farmers and visitors, to make a "frolick" afterwards, called "the largess spending". By way of returning thanks, though perhaps formerly of much more, or of different signification, they immediately leave the seat of festivity and, with the very long and repeated shout of "a largess", the number of shouts being regulated by the sums given, seem to wish to make themselves heard by the people of the surrounding farms. And before they rejoin the company within, the pranks and the jollity I have endeavoured to describe, usually take place. These customs, I believe, are going fast out of use; which is one great reason for my trying to tell the rising race of mankind, that such were the customs when I was a boy. I have annexed a glossary of such words as may be found by general readers to require explanation."

The Earl of Buchan was again very enthusiastic over this publication as were his many friends. Bloomfield seems to have come into contact with nearly all the great figures of the time, and to have endeared himself to most of them including, among others, the then famous Cornish singer, Charles Incledon, and Singleton Copley, the American portrait and historical painter. He was an occasional visitor to the Opera House at Covent Garden, but he was not impressed with Italian humour when he saw *The Prince of Taranto* in 1806, preferring, as he wrote to his friend Rogers, the English opera of *Love in a Village*.

"I am unfashionable enough to declare," he said, "and my whole heart goes with it, that I would rather be the author of such a piece than the proprietor of the Opera House, and all the buildings on this side of the street."

Bloomfield came to know a Mr. Thomas Lloyd Baker and his wife, who lived at Uley in Gloucestershire, and, in 1807, he was invited by Mr. Baker to accompany him and some other friends on a tour of the Wye valley. What a wonderful experience this proved to be! He saw for the first time the beautiful scenery which the hills of the West and Wales provided, and he revelled in it. The journey took ten days in all and he kept a journal of his movements in very fine prose. And what is more he wrote a long poem of four books called *The Banks of Wye* although this was not published until nearly four years later, in 1811. There is so much beauty in this poem that it is difficult to quote from it for fear of destroying any of that beauty. His invocation to Burns, is, however, in itself complete:

"Spirit of Burns! the daring child
Of glorious freedom, rough and wild,
How have I wept o'er all they ills,
How blest thy Caledonian hills!
How almost worshipp'd in my dreams
Thy mountain haunts—thy classic streams!
How burnt with hopeless, aimless fire
To mark thy giant strength aspire
In patriotic themes, and tuned the while
Thy "Bonny Doon" or "Ballock Mile."
Spirit of Burns, accept the tear
That rapture gives thy memory here
On the bleak mountain-top. Here thou
Thyself hadst raised the gallant brow
Of conscious intellect, to twine
Th'imperishable verse of thine
That charms the world. Or can it be
That scenes like these were naught to thee?"

Going down the Wye he saw, for the first time, a coracle of which he recorded his joy in verse.

Much of the beauty of Bloomfield lies in his use of the ordinary words of our language—his simplicity of diction. He is, we think, unrivalled in this particular field for he is able to take, as no other poet except Clare, the commonplace and build it into an edifice of superb grandeur using the simplest of words.

In the fields the gleaners were at work, and of all the delightful love songs which Bloomfield wrote, *Gleaner's Song* is one of the best. Again in it is found that simple language woven into unsurpassed lyrical excellence.

This work is Bloomfield in happy, excited maturity. In his delightful prose diary *Journal of a Tour Down the Wye* he tells of his carefree enjoyment of the expedition:—

"My heart is brimful of indescribable pleasures when I think on this day."

"We spent a delightful and social evening at *The Beaufort Arms*, Chepstow."

On arriving at Tintern Abbey: "Most of the party sat down and took sketches of the interior; but I found it above my reach, so gave vent to my feelings by singing for their amusement and my own the 104th Psalm; and though no "fretted vault" remains to harmonise the sound, it soothed me into the state of mind which is most to be desired."

Among all the excitement and wonderment that filled his conscious hours he found time to write three times to his Mary Anne at home telling her of many of his experiences from day to day and not least of this at Abergavenny—"We came yesterday evening to this town, slept sound, and this morning engaged an old Welshman with a cart with benches, and three little horses, to carry us to the summit of the Sugar-loaf Mountain, such fun, such a road, and such a feast on the mountain moss, and such a sight! I shall talk of it all the rest of my life."

At Ross he called upon an old acquaintance and fellow tradesman, Charles Jones, a shoemaker who lived opposite the *Swan Inn* there. They had worked together in the London garrets. Elsewhere he records this anecdote.

"Charles Jones's brother once lent a shopmate his great coat on a particular occasion. On his return home, this shoemaker declared that he never walked the streets so uncomfortably in his life. Wherever he went, the beggars were after him at every corner and he concluded by protesting that he would not again wear a good coat upon any account whatever. He most likely kept his word, for he was a terrible drunkard."

In conclusion he writes:— "I have imbibed the highest degree of affection for all the individuals of the party, from the most natural cause in the world—because they all seemed glad to give me pleasure, and I shall forget them all when my grave is strewn with flowers."

During the four years or so between the actual journey down the Wye Valley and the publication of the poem which describes it, Bloomfield had a great deal of correspondence regarding it with many people, particularly the Bakers and Samuel Rogers, who thought he should have taken more care over it. Accordingly he wrote the whole out again, and won his friend's approval, but he must needs seek the opinions of two other friends, Mr. Thomas Inskip and Mr. Weston, and also of his first benefactor, Mr. Lofft, as a result of which he wrote the whole out yet again. He was still not entirely satisfied with the result and submitted it to the calm, judicious and candid Mr. Park of Hampstead, who was of the opinion that the thing would do him credit, but at the same time pencilled a few remarks here and there upon it. Bloomfield's final remarks are truly Bloomfieldian: "With this encouragement, I once more wrote out the whole; gave the brat a name; and offered it to my bookseller. I know of nothing which can now retard its ultimate appearance before the world." He was right and it appeared in four books, as he intended it should do, the new

Duke of Grafton being one of the first to receive a copy from the poet himself. It included four ballads, and it was Bloomfield's wish that these should be set to music, and in order to achieve this he sought the aid of no less a person than Mr. William Shield, Master of the King's Musicians. This was one of the few rebuffs he received, for Shield who wrote him a very kindly letter, never found it convenient to meet him, and he was therefore reluctantly obliged to drop the idea.

All his life he was troubled with ill health due to a weakness of constitution. He suffered from terrible headaches, and from dropsy and melancholia. He was never really strong. He wrote some of his best poems when he was under the strange narcotic of pain. Despite all his aches and pains he had a great sense of humour, at times almost whimsical, but always of the very 'dry' Suffolk vintage. For in spite of all the vicissitudes of his worrying life he remained to the end Giles of Suffolk. A few verses written to his friends, Mr. C. Sharp and Mr. Doeg amply illustrate his wit, and humour under stress. He is replying to an invitation to visit Mr. Sharp.

> "I cannot with pleasure leave home,
> Though wit, wine, and friendship invite;
> For my grim-visaged fiend is just come,
> Who withers the germs of delight.
>
> With the vile grin of conquest he rides,
> And demands from its peg my warm coat;
> Deep probing back, shoulders, and sides,
> With a dart—like the name to your note
>
> Your blithe Caledonian for once,
> Whose humour will keep you from sinking,
> Will miss, by good fortune, the dunce
> Who spends his dull moments in thinking.
>
> But should Doeg transgress show the door,
> And let the fine rain cool his flame;
> Or to have him like me make him poor,
> And strike out the e from his name."

His rare prose writings are often, in fact almost always of the same capricious nature. This little-known extract from a letter to Mrs. Baker is a splendid example of his powers in this field. It is no wonder that he was so much sought after at this time.

MISSING

"Whereas on Monday afternoon, an elderly gentleman, remarkable for taciturnity and an unaltered countenance, accompanied his friend from the city to the west end of the town, and has not since been heard of.

The said gentleman is a citizen of respectable appearance wearing a large full-bottomed peruke, which though it has never been combed is as smooth as on the first day it was formed. It is presumed that the said gentleman is not detained from any legal process, nor for any riotous behaviour in the streets, he being never known to be guilty of such misdemeanours, except (as is always the case when kings do wrong) he may have been used as an instrument in the hands of wicked and designing men. And in thus linking the said gentleman to his present most gracious Majesty and other kings, no harm whatever is meant, as in some other particulars he might be likened most truly, particularly this—he speaks not himself, but others speak for him.

The said gentleman has never declared his opinion on politics; but still it is known that he is neither a Jacobin nor a Ministerialist; but it is thought that in the cause of reform, he would in certain cases be of great service. The said gentleman was never instructed in grammar or logic, any more than his friend; yet it is shrewdly suspected that, should his friend be attacked, he would be able to lay down some strong arguments on the side of justice. The said gentleman has sometimes been seen in a cookshop and sometimes in better company; but (what is very important in these times) was never known to eat or drink! which, considering him as a citizen, is perhaps the most extraordinary trait in his character. His backwardness in speaking his own praise will not hinder us from supposing that he has served his country; a large scar on his left cheek seems to confirm this opinion. His complexion, like his friend's, is remarkably dark, and he stoops considerably, which is supposed to proceed from intense study, for, as the said gentleman never wastes his time in idle conversation, it is universally believed that he must know a great deal! Whether he does or not, his friend would be glad to know where he is. In plain English, I left my walking-stick at your house."

In a footnote he explains his anxiety for its recovery, for it had been his constant companion from the time when he began to write *The Farmer's Boy*. "It is one of my valuables", he said.

The years spent in the City Road were undoubtedly some of his happiest. Like a true countryman he loved his garden. He was fully occupied in many other ways, also and not least in that of bringing up and educating his five children, Hannah, Mary Anne, Charles, Charlotte and Robert II (the first Robert having died in infancy) and in making friends with all the great people of his day and age.

Artists sought the privilege of 'making his portrait'. They included such famous men as Rising, Violet, James Northcote, John Hoppner R.A., John Opie, the Cornish wonder whose second wife Amelia he knew so well, and John Young, engraver to H.R.H. the Prince of Wales. It is not certain which of them painted that portrait of his mother during her last long visit to him in 1804. How unfortunate that there is no picture of his beloved Mary Anne, his faithful wife, [Polly was his pet name for her] who, we are told, was very attractive, and who provided the inspiration for many of his effusions on love, and many there are, sparkling like diamonds wherever a human tale is told.

A most unusual and interesting experience took place at this time. A certain young officer at Portsmouth wrote to him anonymously, but giving his address, asking him to write an elegy upon a naval captain, a friend of his, who had died on return from a foreign station. The writer wanted to pass the lament off as his own and offered Bloomfield £5 as a token payment and promised a further £5 on completion. Bloomfield of course sent the money back to him with his refusal saying: "But if this is to pass as a joke, it reminds me of one much better which took place between Dean Swift and Mr. Pope, when the former offered the latter £20 to change his religion."

An apology, which was readily accepted, very soon came from a certain Joseph Banfield who stated that he was a friend of the young officer's father, and begged for his pardon.

He was once invited to attend a ball by a lady who shall be nameless, and who had, as we should say today, 'a crush on him'. He sent her this:—

"May health brace your nerves as I find you're for gadding,
And Care drop the end of his tether,
And stately dame Conscience give license for madding,
And toss up your heart like a feather.

My heart, my good lady, to mirth is no foe,
And many the joys which it feels;
My heart—why it danced thirty summers ago,
But I never could dance with my heels."

5   Move to Bedfordshire

In the early part of the year 1812, when ''bricks and mortar were on the march across the nearby green fields'', when all Europe was again threatened by Napoleon, and the price of food and all necessities were rising on account of the tremendous cost of the Wars, two of his publishers failed in quick succession and he lost at least £500. So in the hope of benefiting his health and lessening his expenses he moved from the City Road to Shefford where he was able to rent a house in Bedford Street, now called North Bridge Street, for £15 per year as opposed to the £40 he was paying in London. His income was shrinking mainly because of his tenderness of heart and great generosity to all and sundry, particularly to his relations in Suffolk, and he was becoming poorer as the years went by. He had purchased the cottage, the ancestral home, at Honington from his brothers and sisters after his mother's death and had allowed Isaac to live there rent free. George and Isaac both drew considerable sums from him from time to time. He lent one of his wife's relatives £100 which was never returned. Not only did these things injure him financially but they depressed him also. Fortunately the new Duke of Grafton had continued to pay him the pension granted him by his father, so with what he received from his writings and from his 'trade', which he was again obliged to follow for a while, and from the aeolian harps he made, he was able to manage.

Why did he not go back to the Suffolk which he loved and where he belonged? There were two reasons. One was that he wanted to get as far away from his near relatives as possible, so that they could not pester him further. There had been so much wrangling among them when he cleared up his mother's affairs after her funeral that on his return to London he vowed never to go back to Honington again. He wrote at that time: "Honington I have done with and it seems effectually to have done with me." The other was that the Bloomfields living in Bury St Edmunds were his cousins and being richer than him they could have caused him some embarrassment. He elected to go to Shefford because of all the people he had come to know through *The Farmer's Boy*, two of them, and very good friends they became, lived there. They were Joseph Weston, who with his sister ran a grocer's and draper's shop in town, and Thomas Inskip. It was from this Joseph Weston that he rented his house for it was to him that he had written in 1811 saying "I have nothing to boast of as to health and appetite. I want to get well under a hedge and I cannot find one to my liking*. My children are growing up round my table, even the pudding would instinctively tell you this if it could talk!"

At this time he also wrote to the new Duke of Grafton concerning his promise to continue his late father's donation to him of fifteen pounds a year. At the end of his letter he says "I would not thus intrude now, had I not determined to live in the country and actually sent my goods and wife and five children to Shefford in Bedfordshire, for I find the expenses of London housekeeping too heavy for my precarious income, and have besides by no means good health."

This is how he describes his new abode when he moved into it: "We have a good house, a middling garden and a rich country on all sides; every charm of spring surrounds us...a robin is building in the meadow behind, the nightingale is heard even to the doors, the cuckoo plies his two notes all day, and a colony of frogs their one by twilight."

He was now in his 46th year and in reasonable spirits. The change had had some beneficial effect upon his mental health at any rate and for the first few years of his stay here he was apparently fairly happy and contented going for walks into the surrounding countryside, engaging in literary reading groups in the evenings, and interesting himself in the "doings" of the little town. Soon after his arrival he penned a delightful little poem called *The Man In The Moon*, which is little known and appears only in the *Fragments* which were collected after his death. It reflected his happier mood at that time.

---

*No doubt on account of the building that was going on round London at that time.

What an eventful year 1812 was to prove for Robert Bloomfield. In April he is happy in the hope of receiving at least £2000 from his copyrights. By September his publishers have gone bankrupt and he finds himself, as he signs himself to his daughter Hannah in a letter written on September 10th, "Your cheated and bamboozled Father".

He was always a great reader, as one would expect, and consequently he had collected a tremendous number of books into a capacious library. He kept himself abreast of the age in which he lived by his daily reading of *The Times*, of which he left the complete issues from 1810 to the end of 1816. One of his delights was to go over to the *Green Man* opposite his home for his drink of ale. Another was the visits he paid to the theatre where the strolling players performed in a malt-house at *The King's Arms*. He particularly mentions Oliver Goldsmith's *She Stoops to Conquer*. Hannah, his eldest and dearest daughter, was a great comfort to him in his last years. And it is to her that we find him writing regularly whenever she is away from home, and it is from these letters that we learn much about his life at Shefford. Gradually his wife, Mary Anne, became obsessed with a strange kind of religious mania and was an avowed follower of the crazy Johanna Southcott who hailed from Devonshire and declared herself to be the woman described in Revelation XII who would give birth to a second Prince of Peace on October 19th, 1814.*

In one of his many letters to Hannah he describes a most unusual dream he has had whilst staying at *The King's Head Inn* at Dover during a tour of the Canterbury area and the north-east Kent coast including Ramsgate, Margate and Folkestone in June 1814. He said: "I am going to relate to you an extraordinary dream from which I am yet scarcely awake, and which fills my mind with unspeakable delight. Methought that I was hurried away to London, which I had so lately left, and told to sleep in the attic storey in Fleet Street, and to visit half the sugar warehouses in the town, climbing up slimy stairs, amidst treacle, figs and barrels of raisins. Soon after I thought I was whirled away 'in the spirit' to Rochester, and had to gaze from the top of the old castle, and tried in vain to encompass the works at Chatham amidst a pouring rain. From thence I was compelled to ride or fly through a fog as thick as the smoke of gunpowder, and was surrounded by tongues speaking everything but what I understood. Nothing ran in my head but French prisoners, and that I was going

---

*Mrs Bloomfield outlived her husband by eleven years. She had become a constant worry to him, particularly in the later years of his life. She died in the Bedford Asylum in 1834 and was buried in the churchyard of St Mary's Church in Bedford.

with them to Dover! Cossacks in bearskins helped to fill the crowded road before us, and I once, for a moment, which is the case with other dreams, saw, as plainly as I ever did awake, the tower of Canterbury Cathedral. After this, night seemed to close in fast, and with my whole company, I was destined to descend steep chalk hills and go headlong into the sea. It was in vain to expostulate with the pale-faced spectre who directed our course. I found myself surrounded with a hubbub of voices and trunks of old clothes, and the roar of the sea beach, mingled with loud discharges of immense artillery placed on the cliffs over our heads. I saw Queen Anne's pocket piece as plain as I ever shall, unless I see it when I am awake. My head was soon after full of music, and I plainly and distinctly heard a band of angels in red coats on a mountain in the clouds, play on trumpets the well-known tune, '*All's Well*'. I then saw the flash of cannon from ships of war in the harbour, which were answered from stupendous heights by the thunder of thirty-two pounders, and a triple fire of an army placed on the beach, whose guns were all directed towards France. In short nothing could exceed the astonishment I felt when I awoke and actually found myself alive and well at *The King's Head Inn* at Dover, where I am now writing with one hand and smoking with the other!''

The national anxiety concerning the threatened invasion by the French seems to have had its effect upon Bloomfield also. And in this connection his short poem addressed to Mrs. Palmer, one of his very great admirers, and the mother of the famous landscape painter, Samuel Palmer, is worthy of note. It was written when he was asked by this lady to repair a bust, a miniature bust of the great Napoleon Buonaparte, which incidentally she gave to him and which he kept until his death, among the books and the other things which she had given him from time to time.

Grief came to him in 1814, when his second daughter Mary Anne died at the age of twenty-one. In a letter to a friend in October of that year he wrote. ''I have buried a daughter who possessed all that I could wish in sense and affection. My wife is a staunch disciple of Johanna Southcott, my four children at home. The eldest boy formerly lame, is growing healthy, and is making a rapid progress in arithmetic. My youngest boy is seven and a half and likewise goes to school. My eldest girl is a woman in years, and, I hope, in all that may continue her my friend. The youngest girl is thirteen and is growing fast.''

Although he did not go back to Suffolk himself, his daughter Hannah used to visit friends in Bury St Edmunds, the Lockwoods, and for a while she took a place with the Westons in a dressmaking business which Mrs. Weston had started at Twickenham, but she was back

(i) Robert Bloomfield 1766-1823

(ii)   Mrs. Elizabeth Bloomfield (née Manby). Robert Bloomfield's mother.

(iii) Sapiston Church where Robert's parents, George and Elizabeth Bloomfield were married on June 1, 1755.

(iv) The Grange, the farm house at Sapiston where William Austin, an Uncle by marriage, offered Robert a home and on whose farms he found employment.

(v) The ford and water mill on the Blackbourne Stream at Sapiston.

(vi) Triangle House, Sapiston a property believed to have been farmed by William Austin and where Robert probably also worked.

(vii)   The cottage at Honington where Robert Bloomfield was born.

(viii)   The old oak table now in Moyses' Hall Museum, Bury St. Edmunds.

John Ayliff

(ix)   A contemporary engraving of Honington Church

(x)   Honington Church in 1971

(xi)   Troston Hall home of Capel Lofft.

home in Shefford by the end of 1817. The next year, however, both Charles and Charlotte left to seek their fortunes in London, Charles to the Royal Foundling Hospital School as a teacher and Charlotte to a milliner's establishment in Cavendish Square.

In 1815 Bloomfield published what might be called a novelette. It had been written 14 years before, in 1801, and was called *The History of Little Davy's New Hat*. But the poet was not a novelist, and although the story is interesting it is certainly only suitable for children and then only for the children of a bye-gone age and not for the sophisticated youngsters of today. This effort was followed in 1818 by two other very short little tales, which were equally unworthy of him. They were *The History of the Chicken and the Horse*, and *The History of the Boy and the Wasp*. 'History' being the then current term for 'story'.

Although his health was now rapidly deteriorating, and his last years were sad ones on this account, he always tried to work and so keep in the public eye. But by 1816 he was in a poor plight not only mentally and physically but also financially. His friends rallied round him and in this year Sir Samuel Egerton Brydges, the heir to the manor of Ixworth-Thorpe, a mile from Honington, launched an appeal to people in the 'higher circles' of East Kent to follow the example of their own kind in Suffolk 'to enter into a subscription to be applied in the purchase of an annuity which may secure independence and comfort to himself and his family during the remainder of his own sickly existence'. At the head of the subscription in Suffolk were the Duke of Norfolk, the Duke of Grafton, the Earl of Bristol, and Lord Rous. At that time Bloomfield refused to accept any money from his well-wishers hoping no doubt, to recover his fortunes, but this was not to be, and by March 1819 he was in desperate need. He wrote to his friend Samuel Rogers asking for £100 of the Suffolk subscription, and telling him of his intention to leave the town of Shefford and return to London, "for here my eldest daughter", Hannah, "who lives with me for my sake far more than for her own, has no employment, and I will not be her hindrance." But this was not to be either, and he remained in Shefford.

Two fragments belonging to this period again show Bloomfield as philosopher. They are his *Sonnet to fifteen Gnats seen dancing in the Sunbeams on January 3* and *Hob's Epitaph*.

In 1822 came *May Day With The Muses*. Upon this May day Sir Ambrose Heigham, now in his eightieth year, decides to invite all the tenants upon his estate to foregather at his mansion, Oakley Hall. There they are to pay their rents in rhyme. Bloomfield got the idea from *The Rambler No*. 82, in which a landowner said: "And as

Alfred received the tribute of the Welsh in wolves' heads, I allowed my tenants to pay their rents in butterflies till I had exhausted the papilionaceous tribe. I then directed them to the pursuit of other animals, and obtained by this easy method, most of the grades of insects which land, air or water can supply. . . .I have, from my own ground, the longest blade of grass upon record, and once accepted as a half-year's rent for a field of wheat, containing more grains than had ever been seen before on a single stem.'' And so the stage is set! It presents Bloomfield with the opportunity to allow his characters to tell their stories in verse to the assembled villagers. There is again something almost Chaucerian about the way in which he weaves these quite ordinary tales of country life into a most fascinating and appealing narrative.

Sir Ambrose is described as a kindly and benevolent old gentleman, beloved and respected by all. Bloomfield draws all his characters, as always, from the countryside he knows so well, and there can be little doubt that here we have a true-to-life picture of the poet's great friend, and patron and benefactor, the Duke of Grafton, and of the countryfolk who lived upon his estate, and that the mansion is no other than Euston Hall itself.

> "Sir Ambrose loved the Muses, and would pay
> Due honours even to the ploughman's lay;
> . . . .
> Time past he had on his paternal ground
> With pride the latent sparks of genius found
> In many a local ballad, many a tale,
> As wild and brief as cowslips in the dale,
> Though unrecorded as the gleams of light
> That vanished in the quietness of night.
> "Why not," he cried, as from the couch he rose
> "To cheer my age and sweeten my repose,
> Why not be just and generous in time,
> And bids my tenants pay their rents in rhyme?
> For one half year they shall.—A feast shall bring
> A crowd of merry faces in the spring.—"

And they came and they did just as Sir Ambrose had hoped they would.

Philip, the farmer's son, tells the story of *The Drunken Father*.

The Oakley gamekeeper recites *The Forester*.

John Armstrong, the shepherd, is responsible for *The Shepherd's Dream* or *The Fairies' Masquerade*.

A veteran soldier from the Peninsular Wars sings the joys of home in *The Soldier's Home.*

Rosamund, Philip's lover, has written *Rosamund's Song of Hope*, which she is too shy to read, but Sir Ambrose asks Philip to do it for her.

Lastly there comes 'a sturdy yeoman, buttoned to the throat' and he recounts the strange tale of *Alfred and Jennet* which proves, so Bloomfield says, that a blind person may fall in love.

There is feasting, merriment and dancing, which continues far into the night—

> "Nor was the lawn clear till the moon arose,
> And on each turret pour'd a brilliant gleam
> Of modest light, that trembled on the stream;
> The owl awoke, but dared not yet complain,
> And banished Silence reassumed her reign."

It is in this work that the trivialities of sentimentality occur more frequently than anywhere else in his writings. It certainly seems that most of this is in a way intentional since the story-tellers were only passionate amateurs and could not be expected to rise to any great poetical heights. The title itself has a wisp of humour about it, and the whole poem is replete with a nostalgic happiness, with Bloomfield, as ever, back in his homeland.

Hazelwood Hall, his one and only drama, was completed and given to the world only a few months before he died in 1823.

In his Advertisement to the Reader he said—

"This little dramatic sketch is not so new as it may appear to be. So long ago as 1805, a gentleman met me on the sands at Worthing, and asked me to his house but I never saw him afterwards. He gave me his address as Mr. Goldhawk, Hazelwood Hall, Leith Hall, Surrey. The names never left my mind and I then thought of trying them in a village tale or drama, which I actually began. The subject has slept ever since, until the publication of my *May Day* last spring, left me leisure and inclination to put it into its present form...... The characters are exclusively villagers, with the exception of Jack Whirlwind through whom I have endeavoured to censure the horrible vice of seducing unguarded females, and then leaving them to scorn and misery."

As he says, the idea came from Surrey, but there can be no doubt that the scenes are in Suffolk, and the simple folk are those he knew so well in his own youth in the Honington district. Time and again throughout his works he demonstrates his great love for his native heath. In this play he even makes one of his characters say, "I never loved this little village half so ardently as when I had been visiting the mountains of Scotland". Hazelwood Hall is most probably no other place than that which he knew as Burnt Hall, the remains of which were, even then, no longer to be seen—only the moat and the rookery around it. And all this despite the fact that he has given the avenue leading to it "a distant view of the sea."

Old Spokeum is a wheelwright, as is his son Joel, who works with him at his craft. A widower, he is cared for by a housekeeper, one Judith. Spokeum is absorbed in the invention of a machine with which to pick hops, and for this reason he earns the nickname "Old Hops". Joel is in love with Mary Maythorn, Mary-up-at-the-Hall, an orphan who has been brought up by Lady Hazelwood together with her own daughter, Emma.

Captain Goldhawk, a retired army officer, and childhood friend of Lady Hazelwood, comes to reside in the village after having spent twenty years in India, and brings with him his manservant Gosling John, who becomes friendly with Betty, one of Squire Morrison's maids, and eventually marries her. There are two unusual but clever love-scenes in the play, one between Joel and Mary and the other between Gosling John and Betty. In this latter, it is Betty who does the wooing. Bloomfield has succeeded in portraying the simple, if awkward lovemaking of the Suffolk swain, who loves but finds difficulty in saying so.

Jack Whirlwind, a fourth cousin of Lady Hazelwood, arrives in great style from London stating that he has come to find himself a wife. One of the shafts of his gig has broken and he has left it at Spokeum's to be repaired. He is a conceited ass and a great bore. He takes a fancy to Mary and attempts to force her into his carriage, but her lover Joel comes along at the right moment and, like the fine fellow he is, gives Whirlwind a sound thrashing.

Mary turns out to be Captain Goldhawk's own daughter, and eventually marries her Joel with her father's blessing. Morrison marries Emma, and Gosling John gets the freehold of a small-holding known as Duke's Bottom. In the script the holding is called Duck's Bottom, but it is easily recognised as the little homestead at the end of Duke's Ride at Euston.

This work must be considered worthy of attention for its unusual literary merit, and particularly because it shows, once again, Bloomfield's skill with the simplest words in our language, and his ability, even in his last days, to produce flashes of excellent dialogue.

60

As there are at least a dozen or more songs in the play it would not be difficult to regard it as an opera not yet tried out.

Betty's song to John Gosling is a masterpiece of rural simplicity and utter naiveté. Her love for him is expressed in the language of the farmyard. She tells him that she is willing to be his wife, and there can be no doubt that he "gets the message".

This is Bloomfield back again on the farm. It is Giles once more! Was there ever such a love poem as this?

Among his *Remains* published in 1824 by his daughter Hannah, with a preface by Mr. Weston and dedicated to the Duke of Grafton, we find a delightful little work entitled *The Birds' and Insects' Post Office*. It is in prose and a fascinating piece of language it is. For the first time since Aesop birds and insects are made to communicate with each other, but this time in writing. In his own words, in the preface, he says, "I have endeavoured to make my winged and creeping correspondents talk in their own character, according to their well-known habits and pursuits."

Bloomfield was a great lover of children and this work was intended primarily for them. There are fifteen letters in all: *From the Magpie to the Sparrow. The Sparrow's Reply. From a young Garden Spider to her Mother. From a young Nightingale to a Wren. From an Earwig deploring the loss of all her children. From the Wild Duck to the Tame Duck. The Tame Duck's Reply. From the Gander to the Turkey-cock. The Dunghill-cock to the Chaffinch. The Blue-bottle Fly to the Grasshopper. The Glow-worm to the Humble-bee. From the Pigeon to the Partridge. The Wood-pigeon to the Owl. The Owl in reply to the Wood-pigeon. From the Swallow in the South of France to the English Robin.*

Unfortunately the poet's aim to extend this series into the world of beasts was never realised for unhappily he deferred this undertaking until the woeful period when his physical and mental health had declined, his spirits become dejected, and his circumstances involved in embarrassment and vexation.

His last years were very sad, for he got into debt on account of his wife's improvidence. Because of this he was no longer able to go out and about and maintain his dignity with the tradespeople of the town, and having failed to find a suitable house in or near London to get away from what he called 'this vile town', Shefford, he did a thing which no doubt hastened his end. He shut himself away from society and remained indoors practically always, and did not even take the walks which he enjoyed so much or go to the inn for his ale. Soon his mental condition deteriorated, and he became almost blind. His wife was a great worry to him. Melancholia seized him, and his last weeks were those of an agonised hypochondriac. During these last weeks his faithful daughter Hannah, was with him and nursed him to the end, which came on August 19th 1823. And then came—

"Delicious sleep! From sleep who could forbear,
With no more guilt than Giles, and no more care."

Joseph Weston, who knew him so well, wrote in *The Remains* published in 1824 "The health of Mr. Bloomfield, which had always been delicate, declined rapidly through the last five years of his life. His general debility was aggravated by very painful and almost constant headaches, which nearly deprived him of sight."

He had made several ineffectual attempts to place some of his children in situations where they could maintain themselves; but owing in part to their ill-health and in part to a constitutional timidity, which seems to characterise the whole family of the Bloomfields, he succeeded with only one.

During the last nine years his regular income, exclusive of a few trifling presents, did not average £100 per annum, and upon this income five weakly persons had to subsist.

It cannot, therefore, excite much surprise if this income proved insufficient or that he was unable to clear accounts with his creditors as he had formerly done. This, however, was the most painful circumstance of all, for he had so great a dread of being treated with incivility, as actually to abstain from the exercise necessary to his health lest in his rambles he might encounter the altered looks of his creditors. It is proper, here, to add that his creditors in general behaved with kindness and with great respect to his feelings.

At length, as a last resource, he resolved to sell his cottage at Honington, the paternal estate in which he was born, and endeared to the whole family by many a tender recollection. The sale was effected, but certain objections arising on the part of the purchaser as to the validity of the title, he found himself involved in new vexations and, in point of fact, never received one sixpence of the money.

These accumulating misfortunes at length depressed his spirits so much, that about six months before his death, he began to complain of great confusion of memory, and felt as if his understanding was entangled. He actually wrote to Bury to certify himself as to the existence of his brother George, of which fact he could not be satisfied by any other means.

About three weeks before his death, this hallucination had so much increased as to leave but few intervals of perfect recollection. He was not, however, 'for years', nor even at all, in such a state as to 'render his death consolatory to his connections', as some have unkindly affirmed.

A letter written to his brother, George, in February 1823 gives a very clear picture of the confused and troubled state of his mind in the months immediately preceding his death:

> Shefford, Beds.
> February 20/1823

Dear George,

I received last night a letter from poor sister Bet, which my daughter will copy for you on a following page. It came to me in about 38 days from Alexandria to New York and from thence across the Atlantic to Liverpool and 200 miles into Bedfordshire. . . . .

But one great cause for my writing now is, that for about a fortnight now I have tried to break from my violent dreams in a morning and for myself to believe that my Elder Brother is Living! And then Isaac comes across my mind, but though I know him to be dead his image is so fresh in my memory as yours. It is a strange feeling and I don't much like it and I wish particularly you would let me see your own handwriting to dispel the illusion, and pull the wool out of my brain, for I am afraid I have been working too hard lately. I know very well there are a wife and bairns living in Well Street, but I cannot find you nor bring you living before my mind's eye. But the mind's eye is sometimes misty—pray write directly. My health is tolerably firm and steady. Honington I have done with, and it seems effectually to have done with me, for the devil a farthing of money can I get in my hour of necessity for all the horrible expense and cost I have sustained.

> Love to Susan and the Bits
> Yours as ever Robert Bloomfield.

P.S. Writing is to me harder than digging was 40 years ago, but my mind, my power of Composition, is as strong and more active than ever it was in my life.

The last letter from his sister Elizabeth in Alexandria, U.S.A., to which he had referred read:—

> Alexandria, U.S.A.,
> January 12th 1823

My dear Brother,

I cannot describe the pleasure your letter gave me. I am in better health though far from well. I believe I told you I had dropsy severely and had to undergo an extreme salination which so unhinged the frame I have never been well since. I have lost the sight of my right eye entirely and the other is very weak. You say party spirit and faction and what is still worse we are imitating the vices and luxuries of Europe at a terrible rate. Formerly you might travel from one end of the Union to the other through woods and bye roads without danger, and now the papers are every day giving accounts of robberies murders etc.

So your poor old King is travelling in his old age to gain popularity, but I feel he begins too late. I wish he could see how some of our papers handle him, they do not scruple to insinuate the poor Queen's death was hastened etc.........

Mr. Hingston holds his health well for his age; he was glad to hear from you and wonders you do not write, it's now more than 3 years since we heard from you.

Give my love to all enquiring friends, write soon. I must bid you adieu I cannot write much at a time.

Yours

Elizabeth Hingston

In his pocket, after death, these lines were found, showing that he died as he lived, a God-fearing man, but one with an intense love of nature and the countryside.

> "It is the voice thou gav'st me, God of love,
> And all I see and feel still bears thy sway,
> And when the Spring breaks forth on mead and grove
> Thou art my God! Thou are the God of May."

He was buried in the Churchyard of Campton, a nearby village, in keeping with the wishes he expressed in his poem *Love of Country* written some 20 years earlier, which ends:

> "O Heaven, permit that I may lie
> Where o'er my corse green branches wave;
> And those, who from life's tumult fly,
> With kindred feelings press my grave."

A tombstone was erected to mark his resting place, by his friend, Thomas Inskip, who was eventually buried beside him.

His dying wish was that his memorial should be written by either of these two of his friends, Thomas Park or Robert Southey, a wish that was never fulfilled. Park was unable to undertake the task on account of ill-health and Southey, while not refusing to do the work or regarding it as unimportant, in fact he is distinctly recorded as having spoken to the contrary, was so much pressed by other and closer engagements, for he was at this time Poet Laureate, that the job was never tackled.

Bloomfield was an exemplary character. His anxious care for others dominated his whole outlook on life. He was a model son, husband, brother and father, and even son-in-law, for he took his father-in-law Church to live with him in his old age. He was generous to a fault, and his anxiety for his family was one of the causes for his early decline both mentally and physically as well as financially. In the words of a twentieth-century kinsman of his, the Rev. Harry Bloomfield, "Robert himself might have been a rich man but for the fact that his brothers and sisters and all their children constantly worried him with their importunity. He practically kept them all and so impoverished himself."

When in health he was a good companion, and his company was much sought after. He was, according to Capel Lofft, a born raconteur with a great sense of humour. He would often recount the story of the Suffolk boy who, going into Essex to see his uncle, and looking up at the moon said, "La, uncle! why your Essex moon is just like our Suffolk moon." He could sing and he could draw, being particularly good at quick sketches of people. Of his contemporaries, the man closest to him in his peasant origins, and his love of nature, was John Clare of Northamptonshire, and after Clare he is most akin to Wordsworth in that he was able to rise to great poetical heights, and also to descend to the mediocre. But it must again be emphasised that he was the master in the subtle use of the simple word, and that there are few if any poets who have been able to make the everyday words of the ordinary man do so much work and at the same time ring so well upon the ear.

Clare and Bloomfield never met although they admired each other from afar, and exchanged 'volumes' and wrote at least once. Bloomfield's letter to Clare runs thus—

"Neighbour John,

If we were still nearer neighbours I would see you and thank you personally for the two volumes of your poems sent to me so long ago. I write with such labour and difficulty that I cannot venture to praise or discriminate like a critic, but must only say that you have given us much pleasure.

I beg your acceptance of my just-published little volume* and sick and ill as I continually feel I can join you heartily in your exclamation: "What is life?"

---

*Probably *May Day with The Muses*.

When Clare heard of Bloomfield's death, he expressed great regret that he had not made his contemplated journey to Shefford to see him and observed: "I deeply regret that ill-health prevented our correspondence and that death prevented us from being better acquainted. I sincerely loved the man and admired his genius." And in his diary he made this entry, "I have desires to know something of Bloomfield's latter days, but I can hear nothing further than his dying neglected, so it's of no use enquiring further, for we know that to be the common lot of genius."

There were so many great writers living at the period when Bloomfield, himself, was alive that it is very surprising that he was able, from his humble position, to make such a tremendous impact upon the literary life of his times. For twenty years and more his works were being published and re-published in almost every part of this country and in the U.S.A. and France. And he was in competition with such people as Samuel Taylor Coleridge, William Wordsworth, Robert Burns, Leigh Hunt, Byron, Keats and Shelley. In addition there were Richard Brinsley Sheridan, Sir Walter Scott, Jane Austen, Anna Barbauld, George Crabbe, Thomas Campbell and Charles Lamb to name but a few. Edmund Blunden of our own times had this to say of Bloomfield, which seems to sum up the position most completely:

"Had we in this country been less fertile in poets, we might still be eulogising or at least reading Robert Bloomfield. He can reveal chapters of rustic truth and pastoral triumph previously unimparted."

Epilogue

Over the years several attempts have been made to draw attention
to the life and works of this great Suffolk poet.

After the publication of his *Remains* by his daughter Hannah in 1824,
little was done until 1870, when Mr. W. H. Hart issued his
Selections From The Correspondence of Robert Bloomfield The Suffolk Poet.
which was fairly well received by the academics, but did not appeal
to ordinary folk.

By 1904 the Robert Bloomfield Society had been founded by Miss
Constance Isherwood of Meppershall Rectory who caused a plaque
to be erected outside his house in Bedford Street, now known as
North Bridge Street, Shefford. It was dedicated on August 19th of that
year and stated very simply:

> "Robert Bloomfield, The pastoral Poet,
> died here, August 19th 1823."
> Erected by Constance Isherwood
> Meppershall Rectory — 1904"

Some twelve years later this same lady, now Mrs MacFarlane, was
instrumental in getting a 'brass' fixed in Honington Church, to
commemorate the 150th anniversary of his birth. It was in the
shape of a shield with this inscription upon it:

Floreat Ager.

In loving memory of Robert Bloomfield, the Suffolk Pastoral Poet, who was born in Honington on December 3rd 1766, and died at Bloomfield House in Shefford, Bedfordshire, on August 19th 1823 aged 57 years, and he rests in Campton Church Bedfordshire.

This tablet was placed here in honour of the 150th anniversary of the poet's birth, on Dec. 3rd 1916 by the President and founders of the Robert Bloomfield Society, Mrs. Constance MacFarlane, and the Vice-Presidents, members and friends of the Society, in grateful remembrance of the pleasures they have ever received from his peerless pastoral poems, full of the love of Nature and his fellow men. (The Farmer's Boy, Rural Tales, Wild Flowers, Good Tidings From the Farm and May Day With The Muses) and also in heartfelt admiration for the beauty and purity of his life and his fine example of kindliness, generosity and sweet sympathy.

"Heaven bless his memory—Bless his honoured name,
He looked from Nature up to Nature's God."

The tablet was unveiled by a kinsman, Mr. A. S. Bloomfield of Coney Weston, whose descendants still live in that neighbouring village of Suffolk.

The bi-centenary of his birth was celebrated with great pomp and ceremony at Honington on December 3rd 1966. Early on that memorable morning the old bell in the turret of the village school was rung 200 times, and by half-past ten a large crowd of villagers and many notable people including one Bloomfield, who had made the journey from far-away-places, had gathered outside the cottage where he was born. There young Robert Jones, himself not unlike in appearance some of the portraits of the poet, dressed as a town crier and shouting "Oyez! Oyez!" declared that this was where Robert Bloomfield was born in 1766. The assembly then moved into the nearby churchyard to the graves of his parents, upon which wreaths were laid by Mr. S. Thurlow, Chairman of the Honington Parish Council. And on to the School Hall where a new portrait of Bloomfield, which had been painted by Mr. L. G. Ives, the Art Master at the school, was unveiled. A Thanksgiving Service was conducted by the Rev. W. Harris, Rector of Honington-with-Sapiston. Bunyan's Pilgrim Hymn *He Who Would Valiant Be*, a connection with Bedfordshire, and the pastoral hymn *All Things Bright and Beautiful* were sung.

The Head Boy of the school, David Pritchard, read "Let us now praise famous men" from Ecclesiasticus, and Kay Watson, Head Girl, born at Fakenham, recited Bloomfield's *The Fakenham Ghost*. After the author William Wickett had paid a tribute to Bloomfield and given a brief resumé of his life, a special bi-centenary song *Two Hundred Years Ago* was sung.

The homage to Bloomfield was still incomplete, for he himself, was lying away at Campton in Bedfordshire, so the following summer a party of over a hundred children, together with their teachers, made a pilgrimage to that place, where they each laid a bunch of flowers upon his grave.

THE FARMER'S BOY

SPRING

O Come, blest Spirit! whatsoe'er thou art,
Thou rushing warmth that hover'st round my heart,
Sweet inmate, hail! thou source of sterling joy,
That poverty itself cannot destroy,
Be thou my Muse; and, faithful still to me,
Retrace the paths of wild obscurity.
No deeds of arms my humble lines rehearse;
No Alpine wonders thunder through my verse,
The roaring cataract, the snow-topt hill,
Inspiring awe, till breath itself stands still:
Nature's sublimer scenes ne'er charm'd mine eyes,
Nor Science led me through the boundless skies;
From meaner objects far my raptures flow;
O point these raptures! bid my bosom glow!
And lead my soul to ecstasies of praise
For all the blessings of my infant days!
Bear me through regions where gay Fancy dwells;
But mould to Truth's fair form what Memory tells.

Live, trifling incidents, and grace my song,
That to the humblest menial belong:

To him whose drudgery unheeded goes,
His joys unreckon'd as his cares or woes;
Though joys and cares in every path are sown,
And youthful minds have feelings of their own,
Quick-springing sorrows, transient as the dew,
Delights from trifles, trifles ever new.
'Twas thus with Giles: meek, fatherless and poor:
Labour his portion, but he felt no more;
No stripes, no tyranny his steps pursu'd;
His life was constant, cheerful servitude:
Strange to the world, he wore a bashful look,
The fields his study, Nature was his book;
And, as revolving Seasons chang'd the scene
From heat to cold, tempestuous to serene,
Though every change still varied his employ,
Yet each new duty brought its share of joy.

Where noble Grafton spreads his rich domains,
Round Euston's water'd vale, and sloping plains,
Where woods and groves in solemn grandeur rise,
Where the kite brooding, unmolested flies;
The woodcock and the painted pheasant race,
And skulking foxes, destined for the chace;
There Giles, untaught and unrepining, stray'd
Through every copse, and grove, and winding glade;
There his first thoughts to Nature's charms inclin'd,
That stamps devotion on th' inquiring mind.
A little farm his generous Master till'd,
Who with peculiar grace his station fill'd;
By deeds of hospitality endear'd,
Serv'd from affection, for his worth rever'd;
A happy offspring blest his plenteous board,
His fields were fruitful, and his barns well stor'd,
And fourscore ewes he fed; a sturdy team;
And lowing kine that graz'd beside the stream:
Unceasing industry he kept in view;
And never lack'd a job for Giles to do.

Fled now the sullen murmurs of the North,
The splendid raiment of the Spring peeps forth;
Her universal green, and the clear sky,
Delight still more and more the gazing eye.

Wide o'er the fields, in rising moisture strong,
Shoots up the simple flower, or creeps along
The mellow'd soil; imbibing fairer hues,
Or sweets from frequent showers and evening dews;
That summon from their sheds the slumb'ring plows,
While health impregnates every breeze that blows.
No wheels support the diving, pointed, share;
No groaning ox is doom'd to labour there;
No helpmates teach the docile steed his road;
(Alike unknown the plow boy and the goad;)
But, unassisted through each toilsome day,
With smiling brow the plowman cleaves his way,
Draws his fresh parallels, and, wid'ning still,
Treads slow the heavy dale, or climbs the hill:
Strong on the wing his busy followers play,
Where writhing earth-worms meet th'unwelcome day;
Till all is chang'd, and hill and level down
Assume the livery of sober brown;
Again disturb'd, when Giles with wearying strides
From ridge to ridge the ponderous harrow guides:
His heels deep sinking every step he goes,
Till dirt adhesive loads his clouted shoes.
Welcome green headland! firm beneath his feet;
Welcome the friendly bank's refreshing seat!
There, warm with toil, his panting horses browse,
Their shelt'ring canopy of pendent boughs;
Till rest, delicious, chase each transient pain,
And new-born vigour swell in every vein.
Hour after hour, and day to day succeeds;
Till every clod and deep-drawn furrow spreads
To crumbling mould; a level surface clear,
And strew'd with corn to crown the rising year;
And o'er the whole Giles once transverse again,
In earth's moist bosom buries up the grain.
The work is done; no more to man is given;
The grateful Farmer trusts the rest to Heaven.
Yet oft with anxious heart he looks around,
And marks the first green blade that breaks the ground;
In fancy sees his trembling oats uprun,
His tufted barley yellow with the sun;
Sees clouds propitious shed their timely store,
And all his harvest gather'd round his door.

72

But still unsafe the big swoln grain below,
A fav'rite morsel with the Rook and Crow;
From field to field the flock increasing goes;
To level crops most formidable foes:
Their danger well the wary plunderers know,
And place a watch on some conspicuous bough;
Yet oft the culking gunner by surprise
Will scatter death amongst them as they rise.
These, hung in triumph round the spacious field,
At best will but a short-liv'd terror yield:
Nor guards of property: (not penal law,
But harmless riflemen of rags and straw;)
Familiariz'd to these, they boldly rove,
Nor heed such centinels that never move.
Let then your birds lie prostrate on the earth,
In dying posture, and with wings stretch'd forth;
Shift them at eve or morn from place to place,
And death shall terrify the pilfering race;
In the mid air, while circling round and round,
They call their lifeless comrades from the ground;
With quick'ning wing, and notes of loud alarm,
Warn the whole flock to shun th' impending harm.

   This task had Giles, in fields remote from home:
Oft has he wish'd the rosy morn to come:
Yet never fam'd was he, nor foremost found
To break the seal of sleep; his sleep was sound:
But when at day-break summon'd from his bed,
Light as the lark that carol'd o'er his head.—
His sandy way deep-worn by hasty showers,
O'er-arch'd with oaks that form'd fantastic bow'rs,
Waving aloft their tow'ring branches proud,
In borrow'd tinges from the eastern cloud,
Whence inspiration, pure as ever flow'd,
And genuine transport in his bosom glow'd.
His own shrill matin join'd the various notes
Of Nature's music, from a thousand throats:
The Blackbird strove with emulation sweet,
And Echo answer'd from her close retreat;
The sporting White-throat on some twig's end borne,
Pour'd hymns to freedom and the rising morn;
Stopt in her song perchance the starting Thrush

Shook a white shower from the black-thorn bush,
Where dew-drops thick as early blossoms hung,
And trembled as the minstrel sweetly sung.
Across his path, in either grove to hide,
The timid Rabbit scouted by his side;
Or bold Cock-Pheasant boldly stalk'd along the road,
Whose gold and purple tints alternate glow'd.

But groves no farther fenc'd the devious way;
A wide-extended heath before him lay,
Where on the grass the stagnant shower had run,
And shone a mirror to the rising sun,
Thus doubly seen to light a distant wood,
To give new life to each expanding bud;
And chase away the dewy foot-marks found,
Where prowling Reynard trod his nightly round;
To shun whose thefts 'twas Giles's evening care,
His feather'd victims to suspend in air,
High on the bough that nodded o'er his head,
And thus each morn to strew the field with dead.

His simple errand done, he homeward hies;
Another instantly its place supplies.
The clatt'ring Dairy-Maid immers'd in steam,
Singing and scrubbing midst her milk and cream,
Bawls out, "Go fetch the Cows!"—he hears no more;
For pigs, and ducks, and turkeys, throng the door,
And sitting hens, for constant war prepar'd;
A concert strange to that which late he heard.
Straight to the meadow then he whistling goes;
With well-known halloo calls his lazy Cows:
Down the rich pasture heedlessly they graze,
Or hear the summon with an idle gaze;
For well they know the cow-yard yields no more
Its tempting fragrance, nor its wintry store.
Reluctance marks their steps, sedate and slow;
The right of conquest all the law they know;
The strong press on, the weak by turns succeed,
And one superior always takes the lead;
Is ever foremost, wheresoe'er they stray;
Allow'd precedence, undisputed sway;
With jealous pride her station is maintain'd,

For many a broil that post of honour gain'd.
At home, the yard affords a grateful scene;
For Spring makes e'en a miry cow-yard clean.
Thence from its chalky bed behold convey'd
The rich manure that drenching Winter made,
Which pil'd near home, grows green with many a weed,
A promis'd nutriment for Autumn's seed.
Forth comes the Maid, and like the morning smiles;
The Mistress too, and follow'd close by Giles.
A friendly tripod forms their humble seat,
With pails bright scour'd, and delicately sweet.
Where shadowing elms obstruct the morning ray,
Begins the work, begins the simple lay;
The full-charg'd udder yields its willing streams,
While Mary sings some lover's amorous dreams;
And crouching Giles beneath a neighbouring tree
Tugs o'er his pail, and chants with equal glee;
Whose hat with tatter'd brim, of nap so bare.
From the cow's side purloins a coat of hair,
A mottled ensign of his harmless trade,
An unambitious, peaceable cockade.
As unambitious too that cheerful aid
The Mistress yields beside her rosy Maid;
With joy she views her plenteous reeking store,
And bears a brimmer to the dairy door;
Her Cows dismiss'd, the luscious mead to roam,
Till eve again recall them loaded home.
And now the Dairy claims her choicest care,
And half her household find employment there:
Slow rolls the churn, its load of clogging cream
At once foregoes its quality and name:
From knotty particles first floating wide
Congealing butter's dash'd from side to side;
Streams of new milk through flowing coolers stray,
And snow-white curd abounds, and wholesome whey.
Due north th' unglazed windows, cold and clear,
For warming sunbeams are unwelcome here.
Brisk goes the work beneath each busy hand,
And Giles must trudge, whoever gives command;
A Gibeonite, that serves them all by turns:
He drains the pump, from him the faggot burns;
From him the noisy Hogs demand their food;

While at his heels run many a chirping brood,
Or down his path in expectation stand,
With equal claims upon his strewing hand.
Thus wastes the morn, till each with pleasure sees
The bustle o'er, and press'd the new-made cheese.

Unrivall'd stands thy country Cheese, O Giles!
Whose very name alone engenders smiles;
Whose fame abroad by every tongue is spoke,
The well-known butt of many a flinty joke,
That pass like current coin the nation through;
And, ah! experience proves the satire true.
Provision's grave, thou ever-craving mart,
Dependent, huge Metropolis! where Art
Her poring thousands stows in breathless rooms,
Midst pois'nous smokes, and steams, and rattling looms:
Where Grandeur revels in unbounded stores;
Restraint a slighted stranger at their doors!
Thou, like a whirlpool, drain'st the countries round,
Till London market, London price, resound
Through every town, round every passing load,
And dairy produce throngs the eastern road:
Delicious veal and butter, every hour,
From Essex lowlands, and the banks of Stour;
And further far, where numerous herds repose,
From Orwell's brink, from Waveny, or Ouse.
Hence Suffolk dairy-wives run mad for cream,
And leave their milk with nothing but its name;
Its name derision and reproach pursue,
And strangers tell of "three times skimm'd sky-blue."
To cheese converted, what can be its boast?
What, but the common virtues of a post!
If drought o'ertake it faster than the knife,
Most fair it bids for stubborn length of life,
And, like the oaken shelf whereon 'tis laid,
Mocks the weak efforts of the bending blade;
Or in the hog-trough rests in perfect spite,
Too big to swallow, and too hard to bite.
Inglorious victory! Ye Cheshire meads,
Or Severn's flow'ry dales, where Plenty treads,
Was your rich milk to suffer wrongs like these,
Farewell your pride! farewell renowned cheese!

The skimmer dread, whose ravages alone
Thus turn the meads' sweet nectar into stone.

   Neglected now the early daisy lies;
Nor thou, pale primrose, bloom'st the only prize:
Advancing Spring profusely spreads abroad
Flow'rs of all hues, with sweetest fragrance stor'd;
Where'er she treads, Love gladdens every plain,
Delight on tiptoe bears her lucid train;
Sweet Hope with conscious brow before her flies,
Anticipating wealth from Summer skies;
All Nature feels her renovating sway;
The sheep-fed pasture, and the meadow gay;
And trees and shrubs, no longer budding seen,
Display the new-grown branch of lighter green;
On airy downs the idling shepherd lies,
And sees to-morrow in the marbled skies.
Here then, my soul, thy darling theme pursue,
For every day was Giles a shepherd too.

   Small was his charge: no wilds had they to roam;
But bright enclosures circling round their home.
No yellow-blossom'd furze, nor stubborn thorn,
The heath's rough produce, had their fleeces torn;
Yet, ever roving, ever seeking thee,
Enchanting spirit, dear Variety!
O happy tenants, prisoners of a day!
Releas'd to ease, to pleasure, and to play;
Indulg'd through every field by turns to range,
And taste them all in one continual change.
For though luxuriant their grassy food,
Sheep long confin'd but loathe the present good:
Bleating around the homeward gate they meet,
And starve, and pine, with plenty at their feet.
Loos'd from the winding lane, a joyful throng,
See, o'er yon pasture, how they pour along!
Giles round his boundaries takes his usual stroll;
Sees every pass secur'd, and fences whole;
High fences, proud to charm the gazing eye,
Where many a nestling first essays to fly;
Where blows the woodbine, faintly streak'd with red,
And rests on every bough its tender head;

Round the young ash its twining branches meet,
Or crown the hawthorn with its odour sweet.

Say, ye that know, ye who have felt and seen,
Spring's morning smiles, and soul-enliv'ning green,
Say, did you give the thrilling transport way?
Did your eye brighten, when young Lambs at play
Leap'd o'er your path with animated pride,
Or gaz'd in merry clusters by your side?
Ye who can smile, to wisdom no disgrace,
At the arch meaning of a Kitten's face:
If spotless innocence, and infant mirth,
Excites to praise, or gives reflection birth;
In shades like these pursue your fav'rite joy,
Midst Nature's revels, sports that never cloy.

A few begin a short but vigorous race,
And Indolence abash'd soon flies the place;
Thus challeng'd forth, see thither one by one,
From every side assembling playmates run;
A thousand wily antics mark their stay,
A starting crowd, impatient of delay.
Like the fond dove, from fearful prison freed,
Each seems to say, "Come, let us try our speed!"
Away they scour, impetuous, ardent, strong,
The green turf trembling as they bound along;
Adown the slope, then up the hillock climb,
Where every molehill is a bed of thyme;
There panting stop; yet scarcely can refrain;
A bird, a leaf will set them off again;
Or, if a gale with strength unusual blow,
Scatt'ring the wild-briar roses into snow,
Their little limbs increasing efforts try,
Like the torn flow'r the fair assemblage fly.
Ah, fallen rose! sad emblem of their doom;
Frail as thyself, they perish as they bloom!
Though unoffending Innocence may plead,
Though frantic Ewes may mourn the savage deed,
Their shepherd comes, a messenger of blood,
And drives them bleating from their sports and food.
Care loads his brow, and pity wrings his heart,
For lo! the murd'ring Butcher with his cart,

Demands the firstlings of his flock to die,
And makes a sport of life and liberty!
His gay companions Giles beholds no more;
Clos'd are their eyes, their fleeces drench'd in gore;
Nor can Compassion, with her softest notes,
Withhold the knife that plunges through their throats.

Down, indignation! hence, ideas foul!
Away the shocking image from my soul!
Let kindlier visitants attend my way,
Beneath approaching Summer's fervid ray;
Nor thankless glooms obtrude, nor cares annoy,
Whilst the sweet theme is universal joy.

SUMMER

The Farmer's life displays in every part
A moral lesson to the sensual heart.
Though in the lap of Plenty, thoughtful still,
He looks beyond the present good or ill;
Nor estimates alone one blessing's worth,
From changeful seasons, or capricious earth,
But views the future with the present hours,
And looks for failures as he looks for showers;
For casual as for certain want prepares,
And round his yard the reeking haystack rears;
Or clover, blossom'd lovely to the sight,
His team's rich store through many a wintry night.
What though abundance round his dwelling spreads,
Though ever moist his self-improving meads
Supply his dairy with a copious flood,
And seem to promise unexhausted food;
That promise fails, when buried deep in snow,
And vegetative juices cease to flow.
For this, his plough turns up the destin'd lands,
Whence stormy Winter draws its full demands;
For this, the seed minutely small, he sows,
Whence, sound and sweet, the hardy turnip grows.
But how unlike to April's closing days!
High climbs the Sun, and darts his pow'rful rays;
Whitens the fresh-drawn mould, and pierces through
The cumb'rous clods that tumble round the plough.
O'er heaven's bright azure hence with joyful eyes
The Farmer sees dark clouds assembling rise;
Borne o'er his fields a heavy torrent falls,
And strikes the earth in hasty driving squalls.
"Right welcome down, ye precious drops," he cries;
But soon, too soon, the partial blessing flies.
"Boy, bring thy harrows! try how deep the rain
"Has forced its way." He comes, but comes in vain;
Dry dust beneath the bubbling surface lurks,
And mocks his pains the more, the more he works:
Still, midst huge clods, he plunges on forlorn,
That laugh his harrows and the shower to scorn.
E'en thus the living clod, the stubborn fool,
Resists the stormy lectures of the school,

Till tried with gentler means, the dunce to please,
His head imbibes right reason by degrees:
As when from eve till morning's wakeful hour,
Light, constant rain envinces secret pow'r,
And ere the day resumes its wonted smiles,
Presents a cheerful, easy task for Giles.
Down with a touch the mellow'd soil is laid,
And yon tall crop next claims his timely aid;
Thither well pleas'd he hies, assur'd to find
Wild, trackless haunts, and objects to his mind.

Shot up from broad rank blades that droop below,
The nodding Wheatear forms a graceful bow,
With milky kernels starting full, weigh'd down,
Ere yet the sun hath ting'd its head with brown;
There thousands in a flock, for ever gay,
Loud chirping sparrows welcome on the day,
And from the mazes of the leafy thorn
Drop one by one upon the bending corn.
Giles with a pole assails their close retreats,
And round the grass-grown dewy border beats,
On either side completely overspread,
Here branches bend, there corn o'ertops his head.
Green covert, hail! for through the varying year
No hours so sweet, no scene to him so dear.
Here Wisdom's placid eye delighted sees
His frequent intervals of lonely ease,
And with one ray his infant soul inspires,
Just kindling there her never-dying fires,
Whence solitude derives peculiar charms,
And heaven-directed thought his bosom warms.
Just where the parting bough's light shadows play,
Scarce in the shade, nor in the scorching day,
Stretcht on the turf he lies, a peopled bed,
Where swarming insects creep around his head.
The small dust-colour'd beetle climbs with pain,
O'er the smooth plantain-leaf, a spacious plain!
Thence higher still, by countless steps convey'd,
He gains the summit of a shiv'ring blade,
And flirts his filmy wings, and looks around,
Exulting in his distance from the ground.
The tender speckled moth here dancing seen,

The vaulting grasshopper of glossy green,
And all prolific Summer's sporting train,
Their little lives by various pow'rs sustain.
But what can unassisted vision do?
What, but recoil where most it would pursue;
His patient gaze but finish with a sigh,
When Music waking speaks the sky-lark nigh!
Just starting from the corn, he cheerly sings,
And trusts with conscious pride his downy wings;
Still louder breathes, and in the face of day
Mounts up, and calls on Giles to mark his way.
Close to his eyes his hat he instant bends,
And forms a friendly telescope, that lends
Just aid enough to dull the glaring light,
And place the wand'ring bird before his sight,
That oft beneath a light cloud sweeps along,
Lost for a while, yet pours her varied song:
The eye still follows, and the cloud moves by,
Again he stretches up the clear blue sky;
His form, his motion, undistinguish'd quite,
Save when he wheels direct from shade to light:
E'en then the songster a mere speck became,
Gliding like fancy's bubbles in a dream,
The gazer sees; but yielding to repose,
Unwittingly his jaded eyelids close.
Delicious sleep! From sleep who could forbear,
With no more guilt than Giles, and no more care?
Peace o'er his slumbers waves her guardian wing,
Nor Conscience once disturbs him with a sting;
He wakes refresh'd from every trivial pain,
And takes his pole, and brushes round again.

Its dark-green hue, its sicklier tints all fail,
And ripening Harvest rustles in the gale.
A glorious sight, if glory dwells below,
Where Heaven's munificence makes all the show
O'er every field and golden prospect found,
That glads the Plowman's Sunday-morning's round,
When on some eminence he takes his stand,
To judge the smiling produce of the land.
Here Vanity slinks back, her head to hide:
What is there here to flatter human pride?

The tow'ring fabric, or the dome's loud roar,
And stedfast columns, may astonish more,
Where the charm'd gazer long delighted stays,
Yet trac'd but to the architect the praise;
Whilst here, the veriest clown that treads the sod,
Without one scruple gives the praise to God;
And twofold joys possess his raptur'd mind,
From gratitude and admiration join'd.

Here, midst the boldest triumphs of her worth,
Nature herself invites the reapers forth;
Dares the keen sickle from its twelvemonth's rest,
And gives that ardour which in every breast
From infancy to age alike appears,
When the first sheaf its plumy top uprears.
No rake takes here what Heaven to all bestows—
Children of want, for you the bounty flows!
And every cottage from the plenteous store
Receives a burden nightly at its door.

Hark! where the sweeping scythe now rips along
Each sturdy Mower, emulous and strong,
Whose writhing form meridian heat defies,
Bends o'er his work, and every sinew tries;
Prostrates the waving treasure at his feet,
But spares the rising clover, short and sweet,
Come Health! come, Jollity! light-footed, come;
Here hold your revels, and make this your home.
Each heart awaits and hails you as its own;
Each moisten'd brow, that scorns to wear a frown:
Th' unpeopled dwelling mourns its tenants stray'd;
E'en the domestic, laughing Dairy-Maid
Hies to the Field, the general toil to share.
Meanwhile the Farmer quits his elbow-chair,
His cool brick-floor, his pitcher, and his ease,
And braves the sultry beams, and gladly sees
His gates thrown open, and his team abroad,
The ready group attendant on his word,
To turn the swarth, the quiv'ring load to rear,
Or ply the busy rake, the land to clear.
Summer's light garb itself now cumb'rous grown,
Each his thin doublet in the shade throws down;

Where oft the Mastiff skulks with half-shut eye,
And rouses at the stranger passing by;
Whilst unrestrain'd the social converse flows,
And every breast Love's powerful impulse knows,
And rival wits with more than rustic grace
Confess the presence of a pretty face.

For, lo! encircled there, the lovely Maid,
In youth's own bloom and native smiles array'd;
Her hat awry, divested of her gown,
Her creaking stays of leather, stout and brown;—
Invidious barrier! Why art thou so high,
When the slight covering of her neck slips by,
There half revealing to the eager sight,
Her full, ripe bosom, exquisitely white?
In many a local tale of harmless mirth,
And many a jest of momentary birth,
She bears a part, and as she stops to speak,
Strokes back the ringlets from her glowing cheek.

Now noon gone by, and four declining hours,
The weary limbs relax their boasted pow'rs;
Thirst rages strong, the fainting spirits fail,
And ask the sov'reign cordial, home-brew'd ale:
Beneath some shelt'ring heap of yellow corn
Rests the hoop'd keg, and friendly cooling horn,
That mocks alike the goblet's brittle frame,
Its costlier potions, and its nobler name.
To Mary first the brimming draught is given,
By toil made welcome as the dews of heaven,
And never lip that press'd its homely edge
Had kinder blessings, or a heartier pledge.

Of wholesome viands here a banquet smiles,
A common cheer for all;—e'en humble Giles,
Who joys his trivial services to yield
Amidst the fragrance of the open field;
Oft doom'd in suffocating heat to bear
The cobweb'd barn's impure and dusty air;
To ride in mirky state the panting steed,
Destin'd aloft th' unloaded grain to tread,
Where, in his path as heaps on heaps are thrown,

He rears, and plunges the loose mountain down:
Laborious task! with what delight, when done,
Both horse and rider greet th' unclouded sun!

  Yet by th' unclouded sun are hourly bred
The bold assailants that surround thine head,
Poor, patient Ball! and with insulting wing
Roar in thine ears, and dart the piercing sting:
In thy behalf the crest-wav'd boughs avail
More than thy short-clipt remnant of a tail,
A moving mockery, a useless name,
A living proof of cruelty and shame.
Shame to the man, whatever fame he bore,
Who took from thee what man can ne'er restore,
Thy weapon of defence, they chiefest good,
When swarming flies contending suck thy blood.
Nor thine alone the suff'ring, thine the care,
The fretful Ewe bemoans an equal share;
Tormented into sores, her head she hides,
Or angry sweeps them from her new-shorn sides.
Penn'd in the yard, e'en now at closing day
Unruly Cows with mark'd impatience stay,
And vainly striving to escape their foes,
The pail kick down; a piteous current flows.

  Is't not enough that plagues like these molest?
Must still another foe annoy their rest?
He comes, the pest and terror of the yard,
His full-fledg'd progeny's imperious guard;
The Gander;—spiteful, insolent, and bold,
At the colt's footlock takes his daring hold:
There, serpent-like, escapes a dreadful blow;
And straight attacks a poor defenceless cow:
Each booby Goose th' unworthy strife enjoys,
And hails his prowess with redoubled noise.
Then back he stalks, of self-importance full,
Seizes the shaggy foretop of the Bull,
Till whirl'd aloft he falls: a timely check,
Enough to dislocate his worthless neck!
For lo! of old, he boasts an honour'd wound;
Behold that broken wing that trails the ground!
Thus fools and bravoes kindred pranks pursue;

As savage quite, and oft as fatal too.
Happy the man that foils an envious elf,
Using the darts of spleen to serve himself.
As when by turns the strolling Swine engage
The utmost efforts of the bully's rage,
Whose nibbling warfare on the grunter's side
Is welcome pleasure to his bristly hide;
Gently he stoops, or stretcht at ease along,
Enjoys the insults of the gabbling throng,
That march exulting round his fallen head,
As human victors trample on their dead.

Still Twilight, welcome! Rest, how sweet art thou!
Now eve o'erhangs the western cloud's thick brow:
The far-stretcht curtain of retiring light,
With fiery treasures fraught; that on the sight
Flash from its bulging sides, where darkness lours,
In Fancy's eye, a chain of mould'ring tow'rs;
Or craggy coasts just rising into view,
Mids't jav'lins dire, and darts of streaming blue.

Anon tir'd labourers bless their shelt'ring home,
When Midnight, and the frightful Tempest come.
The Farmer wakes, and sees, with silent dread,
The angry shafts of Heaven gleam round his bed;
The bursting cloud reiterated roars,
Shakes his straw roof, and jars his bolted doors:
The slow-wing'd storm along the troubled skies
Spreads its dark course; the wind begins to rise;
And full-leaf'd elms, his dwelling's shade by day,
With mimic thunder give its fury way:
Sounds in his chimney-top a doleful peal
Midst pouring rain, or gusts of rattling hail;
With tenfold danger low the tempest bends,
And quick and strong the sulph'rous flame descends:
The frighten'd Mastiff from his kennel flies,
And cringes at the door with piteous cries.

Where now's the trifler? where the child of pride?
These are the moments when the heart is try'd!
Nor lives the man, with conscience e'er so clear,
But feels a solemn, reverential fear;

Feels too a joy relieve his aching breast,
When the spent storm hath howl'd itself to rest.
Still, welcome beats the long-continued show'r,
And sleep protracted, comes with double pow'r;
Calm dreams of bliss bring on the morning sun,
For every barn is fill'd, and Harvest done!

Now, ere sweet Summer bids its long adieu,
And winds blow keen where late the blossom grew,
The bustling day and jovial night must come,
The long-accustom'd feast of Harvest-Home.
No blood-stain'd victory, in story bright,
Can give the philosophic mind delight;
No triumph please, while rage and death destroy:
Reflection sickens at the monstrous joy.
And where the joy, if rightly understood,
Like cheerful praise for universal good?
The soul nor check nor doubtful anguish knows,
But free and pure the grateful current flows.

Behold the sound oak table's massy frame
Bestride the kitchen floor! the careful dame,
And gen'rous host invite their friends around,
For all that clear'd the crop, or till'd the ground,
Are guests by right of custom:—old and young;
And many a neighbouring yeoman join the throng,
With artizans that lent their dext'rous aid,
When o'er each field the flaming sun-beams play'd.

Yet Plenty reigns, and from her boundless hoard,
Though not one jelly trembles on the board,
Supplies the feast with all that sense can crave;
With all that made our great forefathers brave,
Ere the cloy'd palate countless flavours try'd,
And cooks had Nature's judgment set aside.
With thanks to Heaven, and tales of rustic lore,
The mansion echoes when the banquet's o'er;
A wider circle spreads, and smiles abound,
As quick the frothing horn performs its round;
Care's mortal foe; that sprightly joys imparts
To cheer the frame and renovate their hearts.
Here, fresh and brown, the hazel's produce lies

In tempting heaps, and peals of laughter rise,
And crackling Music, with the frequent Song,
Unheeded bear the midnight hour along.

Here once a year Distinction low'rs its crest,
The master, servant, and the merry guest,
Are equal all; and round the happy ring
The reaper's eyes exulting glances fling,
And, warm'd with gratitude, he quits his place,
With sun-burnt hands and ale-enliven'd face,
Refills the jug his honour'd host to tend,
To serve at once the master and the friend;
Proud thus to meet his smiles, to share his tale,
His nuts, his conversation, and his ale.

Such were the days,—of days long past I sing,
When Pride gave place to mirth without a sting;
Ere tyrant customs strength sufficient bore
To violate the feelings of the poor;
To leave them distanc'd in the madd'ning race,
Where'er refinement shows its hated face:
Nor causeless hated;—'tis the peasant's curse,
That hourly make his wretched station worse;
Destroys life's intercourse; the social plan
That rank to rank cements, as man to man:
Wealth flows around him, Fashion lordly reigns;
Yet poverty is his, and mental pains.

Methinks I hear the mourner thus impart
The stifled murmurs of his wounded heart:
'Whence comes this change, ungracious, irksome, cold?
'Whence the new grandeur that mine eyes behold?
'The widening distance which I daily see,
'Has Wealth done this?—then Wealth's a foe to me:
'Foe to our rights; that leaves a powerful few
'The paths of emulation to pursue:—
'For emulation stoops to us no more:
'The hope of humble industry is o'er;
'The blameless hope, the cheering sweet presage
'Of future comforts for declining age.
'Can my sons share from this paternal hand
'The profits with the labours of the land?

'No; though indulgent Heaven its blessing deigns,
'Where's the small farm to suit my scanty means?
'Content, the Poet sings, with us resides;
'In lonely cots like mine, the Damsel hides;
'And will he then in raptur'd visions tell
'That sweet Content with Want can never dwell?
'A barley loaf, 'tis true, my table crowns,
'That, fast diminishing in lusty rounds,
'Stops Nature's cravings; yet her sighs will flow
'From knowing this,—that once it was not so.
'Our annual feast, when Earth her plenty yields,
'When crown'd with boughs the last load quits the fields,
'The aspect still of ancient joy puts on;
'The aspect only, with the substance gone:
'The self-same Horn is still at our command,
'But serves none now but the plebeian hand:
'For home-brew'd Ale, neglected and debas'd,
'Is quite discarded from the realms of taste.
'Where unaffected Freedom charm'd the soul,
'The separate table and the costly bowl,
'Cool as the blast that checks the budding Spring,
'A mockery of gladness round them fling.
'For oft the Farmer, ere his heart approves,
'Yields up the custom which he dearly loves:
'Refinement forces on him like a tide;
'Bold innovations down its current ride,
'That bear no peace beneath their showy dress,
'Nor add one tittle to his happiness.
'His guests selected; rank's punctilios known;
'What trouble waits upon a casual frown!
'Restraint's foul manacles his pleasures maim;
'Selected guests selected phrases claim:
'Nor reigns that joy, when hand in hand they join,
'That good old Master felt in shaking mine.
'Heaven bless his memory! bless his honour'd name!
'(The poor will speak his lasting worthy fame:)
'To souls fair-purpos'd strength and guidance give;
'In pity to us still let goodness live:
'Let labour have its due! my cot shall be
'From chilling want and guilty murmurs free.
'Let labour have its due; then peace is mine,
'And never, never shall my heart repine.'

AUTUMN

Again, the year's decline, midst storms and floods,
The thund'ring chase, the yellow fading woods,
Invite my song; that fain would boldly tell
Of upland coverts, and the echoing dell,
By turns resounding loud, at eve and morn
The swineherd's halloo, or the huntsman's horn.

No more the fields with scatter'd grain supply
The restless wandering tenants of the Sty;
From oak to oak they run with eager haste,
And wrangling share the first delicious taste
Of fallen Acorns; yet but thinly found
Till the strong gale has shook them to the ground.
It comes; and roaring woods obedient wave:
Their home well pleas'd the joint adventurers leave:
The trudging Sow leads forth her numerous young,
Playful, and white, and clean, the briars among,
Till briars and thorns increasing fence them round,
Where last year's mould'ring leaves bestrew the ground,
And o'er their heads, loud lash'd by furious squalls,
Bright from their cups the rattling treasure falls;
Hot, thirsty food; whence double sweet and cool
The welcome margin of some rush-grown pool,
The Wild Duck's lonely haunt, whose jealous eye
Guards every point; who sits prepar'd to fly,
On the calm bosom of her little lake,
Too closely screen'd for ruffian winds to shake;
And as the bold intruders press around,
At once she starts, and rises with a bound:
With bristles rais'd the sudden noise they hear,
And ludicrously wild, and wing'd with fear,
The herd decamp with more than swinish speed,
And snorting dash through sedge, and rush, and reed:
Through tangling thickets headlong on they go,
Then stop and listen for their fancied foe;
The hindmost still the growing panic spreads,
Repeated fright the first alarm succeeds,
Till Folly's wages, wounds and thorns, they reap:
Yet glorying in their fortunate escape,
Their groundless terrors by degrees soon cease,

And Night's dark reign restores their wonted peace.
For now the gale subsides, and from each bough
The roosting Pheasant's short but frequent crow
Invites to rest; and huddling side by side,
The herd in closest ambush seek to hide;
Seek some warm slope with shagged moss o'erspread,
Dry'd leaves their copious covering and their bed;
In vain may Giles, through gath'ring glooms that fall,
And solemn silence, urge his piercing call:
Whole days and nights they tarry midst their store,
Nor quit the woods till oaks can yield no more.

    Beyond bleak Winter's rage, beyond the Spring
That rolling Earth's unvarying course will bring,
Who tills the ground looks on with mental eye,
And sees next Summer's sheaves and cloudless sky;
And even now, whilst Nature's beauty dies,
Deposits Seed, and bids new Harvests rise;
Seed well prepar'd, and warm'd with glowing lime,
'Gainst earth-bred grubs, and cold, and lapse of time:
For searching frosts and various ills invade,
Whilst wintry months depress the springing blade.
The plough moves heavily, and strong the soil,
And clogging harrows with augmented toil
Dive deep: and clinging, mixes with the mould
A fatt'ning treasure from the nightly fold,
And all the cow-yard's highly valu'd store,
That late bestrew'd the blacken'd surface o'er.
No idling hours are here, when Fancy trims
Her dancing taper over outstretcht limbs,
And in her thousand thousand colours drest,
Plays round the grassy couch of noontide rest:
Here Giles for hours of indolence atones
With strong exertion, and with weary bones,
And knows no leisure; till the distant chime
Of Sabbath bells he hears at sermon time,
That down the brook sound sweetly in the gale,
Or strike the rising hill, or skim the dale.

    Nor his alone the sweets of ease to taste:
Kind rest extends to all:—save one poor beast,
That true to time and pace, is doom'd to plod,

To bring the Pastor to the House of God:
Mean structure; where no bones of heroes lie!
The rude inelegance of poverty
Reigns here alone: else why that roof of straw?
Those narrow windows with the frequent flaw?
O'er whose low cells the dock and mallow spread,
And rampant nettles lift the spiry head,
Whilst from the hollows of the tower on high
The gray capp'd Daws in saucy legions fly.

Round these lone walls assembling neighbours meet,
And tread departed friends beneath their feet;
And new-briar'd graves, that prompt the secret sigh,
Show each the spot where he himself must lie.

Midst timely greetings village news goes round,
Of crops late shorn, or crops that deck the ground;
Experienc'd ploughmen in the circle join;
While sturdy boys, in feats of strength to shine,
With pride elate, their young associates brave
To jump from hollow-sounding grave to grave;
Then close consulting, each his talent lends
To plan fresh sports when tedious service ends.

Hither at times, with cheerfulness of soul,
Sweet village Maids from neighbouring hamlets stroll,
That like the light heel'd does, o'er lawns that rove,
Look shyly curious; rip'ning into love;
For love's their errand: hence the tints that glow
On either cheek, a heighten'd lustre know:
When, conscious of their charms, e'en Age looks sly,
And rapture beams from Youth's observant eye.

The Pride of such a party, Nature's pride,
Was lovely Poll;* who innocently try'd,
With hat of airy shape and ribbons gay,
Love to inspire, and stand in Hymen's way:
But, ere her twentieth Summer could expand,
Or youth was render'd happy with her hand,
Her mind's serenity, her peace was gone,
Her eye grew languid, and she wept alone:

---

*Mary Rayner of Ixworth Thorpe.

Yet causeless seem'd her grief; for quick restrain'd,
Mirth follow'd loud; or indignation reign'd:
Whims wild and simple led her from her home,
The heath, the common, or the fields to roam:
Terror and joy alternate rul'd her hours;
Now blithe she sung, and gather'd useless flow'rs;
Now pluck'd a tender twig from every bough,
To whip the hov'ring demons from her brow.
Ill-fated Maid! thy guiding spark is fled,
And lasting wretchedness awaits thy bed—
Thy bed of straw! for mark, where even now
O'er their lost child afflicted parents bow;
Their woe she knows not, but perversely coy,
Inverted customs yield her sullen joy;
Her midnight meals in secrecy she takes,
Low mutt'ring to the moon, that rising breaks
Thro' night's dark gloom:—oh how much more forlorn
Her night, that knows of no returning morn!—
Slow from the threshold, once her infant seat,
O'er the cold earth she crawls to her retreat;
Quitting the cot's warm walls, unhous'd to lie,
Or share the swine's impure and narrow sty;
The damp night-air her shiv'ring limbs assails:
In dreams she moans, and fancied wrongs bewails.
When morning wakes, none earlier rous'd than she,
When pendant drops fall glitt'ring from the tree;
But nought her rayless melancholy cheers,
Or soothes her breast, or stops her streaming tears.
Her matted locks unornamented flow;
Clasping her knees, and waving to and fro;—
Her head bow'd down, her faded cheek to hide;—
A piteous mourner by the pathway side.
Some tufted molehill through the livelong day
She calls her throne; there weeps her life away:
And oft the gaily-passing stranger stays
His well-tim'd step, and takes a silent gaze,
Till sympathetic drops unbidden start,
And pangs quick-springing muster round his heart;
And soft he treads with other gazers round,
And fain would catch her sorrow's plaintive sound.
One word alone is all that strikes the ear,
One short, pathetic, simple word,—"Oh dear!"

A thousand times repeated to the wind,
That wafts the sigh, but leaves the pang behind!
For ever of the proffer'd parley shy,
She hears th' unwelcome foot advancing nigh;
Nor quite unconscious of her wretched plight,
Gives one sad look, and hurries out of sight—

Fair promis'd sunbeams of terrestrial bliss,
Health's gallant hopes,—and are ye sunk to this?
For in life's road, though thorns abundant grow,
There still are joys poor Poll can never know;
Joys which the gay companions of her prime
Sip, as they drift along the stream of time:
At eve to hear beside their tranquil home
The lifted latch, that speaks the lover come:
That love matur'd, next playful on the knee
To press the velvet lips of infancy;
To stay the tottering step, the features trace;—
Inestimable sweets of social peace!

O Thou, who bidd'st the vernal juices rise!
Thou, on whose blasts autumnal foliage flies!
Let peace ne'er leave me, nor my heart grow cold,
Whilst life and sanity are mine to hold.

Shorn of their flow'rs that shed th' untreasur'd seed,
The withering pasture, and the fading mead,
Less tempting grown, diminish more and more,
The dairy's pride; sweet Summer's flowing store.
New cares succeed, and gentle duties press,
Where the fire-side, a school of tenderness,
Revives the languid chirp, and warms the blood
Of cold-nipt weaklings of the latter brood,
That from the shell just bursting into day,
Through yard or pond pursue their vent'rous way.

Far weightier cares and wider scenes expand;
What devastation marks the new-sown land!
"From hungry woodland foes go, Giles, and guard
The rising wheat: ensure its great reward:
A future sustenance, a Summer's pride,
Demand thy vigilance: then be it try'd:

Exert thy voice, and wield thy shotless gun:
Go tarry there from morn till setting sun."

Keen blows the blast, or ceaseless rain descends;
The half-stript hedge a sorry shelter lends.
O for a Hovel, e'er so small or low,
Whose roof, repelling winds and early snow,
Might bring home's comforts fresh before his eyes!
No sooner thought, than see the structure rise,
In some sequester'd nook, embank'd around,
Sods for its walls, and straw in burdens bound,
Dried fuel hoarded is his richest store,
And circling smoke obscures his little door:
Whence creeping forth, to duty's call he yields,
And strolls the Crusoe of the lonely fields.
On whitethorns tow'ring, and the leafless rose,
A frost-nipt feast in bright vermilion glows;
Where clust'ring sloes in glossy order rise,
He crops the loaded branch; a cumb'rous prize:
And o'er the flame the sputt'ring fruit he rests,
Placing green sods to seat the coming guests;
His guests by promise; playmates young and gay:—
But ah! fresh pastimes lure their steps away!
He sweeps his hearth, and homeward looks in vain,
Till feeling Disappointment's cruel pain.
His fairy revels are exchang'd for rage,
His banquet marr'd, grown dull his hermitage.
The field becomes his prison, till on high
Benighted birds to shades and coverts fly.
Midst air, health, daylight, can he prisoner be?
If fields are prisons, where is Liberty?
Here still she dwells, and here her votaries stroll;
But disappointed hope untunes the soul:
Restraints unfelt whilst hours of rapture flow,
When troubles press, to chains and barriers grow.
Look then from trivial up to greater woes;
From the poor bird-boy with his roasted sloes,
To where the dungeon'd mourner heaves the sigh;
Where not one cheering sun-beam meets his eye.
Though ineffectual pity thine may be,
No wealth, no pow'r, to set the captive free;
Though only to thy ravish'd sight is given

The radiant path that Howard trod to heaven;
Thy slights can make the wretched more forlorn,
And deeper drive affliction's barbed thorn.
Say not, "I'll come and cheer thy gloomy cell
With news of dearest friends; how good, how well:
I'll be a joyful herald to thine heart;"
Then fail, and play the worthless trifler's part,
To sip flat pleasures from thy glass's brim,
And waste the precious hour that's due to him.
In mercy spare the base, unmanly blow:
Where can he turn, to whom complain of you?
Back to past joys in vain his thoughts may stray,
Trace and retrace the beaten, worn-out way,
The rankling injury will pierce his breast,
And curses on thee break his midnight rest.

    Bereft of song, and ever-cheering green,
The soft endearments of the Summer scene,
New harmony pervades the solemn wood,
First heard from kennel bursting, mad with joy,
Dear to the soul, and healthful to the blood:
For bold exertion follows on the sound
Of distant Sportsmen, and the chiding Hound;
Where smiling Euston boasts her good Fitzroy,
Lord of pure alms, and gifts that wide extend;
The farmer's patron, and the poor man's friend:
Whose Mansion glitters with the eastern ray,
Whose elevated temple points the way,
O'er slopes and lawns, the park's extensive pride,
To where the victims of the chase reside,
Ingulf'd in earth, in conscious safety warm,
Till lo! a plot portends their coming harm.

    In earliest hours of dark and hooded morn,
Ere yet one rosy cloud bespeaks the dawn,
Whilst far abroad the Fox pursues his prey,
He's doom'd to risk the perils of the day,
From his strong-hold block'd out; perhaps to bleed,
Or owe his life to fortune or to speed.
For now the pack, impatient rushing on,
Range through the darkest coverts one by one;
Trace every spot; whilst down each noble glade

That guides the eye beneath a changeful shade,
The loit'ring sportsman feels th' instinctive flame,
And checks his steed to mark the springing game.
Midst intersecting cuts and winding ways
The huntsman cheers his dogs, and anxious strays
Where every narrow riding, even shorn,
Gives back the echo of his mellow horn:
Till fresh and lightsome, every pow'r untried,
The starting fugitive leaps by his side,
His lifted fingers to his ear he plies,
And the view-halloo bids a chorus rise
Of Dogs quick-mouth'd, and shouts that mingle loud
As bursting thunder rolls from cloud to cloud.
With ears erect, and chest of vig'rous mould,
O'er ditch, o'er fence, unconquerably bold,
The shining courser lengthens every bound,
And his strong foot-locks suck the moisten'd ground,
As from the confines of the wood they pour,
And joyous villages partake the roar.
O'er heath far stretch'd, or down, or valley low,
The stiff-limb'd peasant, glorying in the show,
Pursues in vain; where Youth itself soon tires,
Spite of the transports that the chase inspires;
For who unmounted long can charm the eye,
Or hear the music of the leading cry?

   Poor faithful Trouncer! thou canst lead no more;
All thy fatigues and all thy triumphs o'er!
Triumphs of worth, whose long-excelling fame
Was still to follow true the hunted game!
Beneath enormous oaks, Britannia's boast,
In thick, impenetrable coverts lost,
When the warm pack in falt'ring silence stood,
Thine was the note that rous'd the list'ning wood,
Rekindling every joy with tenfold force,
Through all the mazes of the tainted course.
Still foremost thou the dashing stream to cross,
And tempt along the animated horse;
Foremost o'er fen or level mead to pass,
And sweep the show'ring dew-drops from the grass;
Then bright emerging from the mist below
To climb the woodland hill's exulting brow.

Pride of thy race! with worth far less than thine,
Full many human leaders daily shine!
Less faith, less constancy, less gen'rous zeal!—
Then no disgrace my humble verse shall feel,
Where not one lying line to riches bows,
Or poison'd sentiments from rancour flows;
Nor flowers are strewn around Ambition's car:
An honest Dog's a nobler theme by far.
Each sportsman heard the tidings with a sigh,
When Death's cold touch had stopt his tuneful cry;
And though high deeds, and fair exalted praise,
In memory liv'd, and flow'd in rustic lays,
Short was the strain of monumental woe:
"Foxes rejoice! here buried lies your foe."*
In safety hous'd throughout Night's length'ning reign,
The Cock sends forth a loud and piercing strain;
More frequent, as the glooms of midnight flee,
And hours roll round that brought him liberty,
When Summer's early dawn, mild, clear, and bright,
Chas'd quick away the transitory night:—
Hours now in darkness veil'd; yet loud the scream
Of Geese impatient for the playful stream;
And all the feather'd tribe imprison'd raise
Their morning notes of inharmonious praise;
And many a clamorous Hen and cockrel gay,
When daylight slowly through the fog breaks way,
Fly wantonly abroad: but, ah, how soon
The shades of twilight follow hazy noon,
Shortn'ing the busy day!—day that slides by
Amidst th' unfinish'd toils of Husbandry;
Toils still each morn resum'd with double care,
To meet the icy terrors of the year;
To meet the threats of Boreas undismay'd,
And Winter's gathering frowns and hoary head.

Then welcome, Cold; welcome, ye snowy nights!
Heaven midst your rage shall mingle pure delights,
And confidence of hope the soul sustain,
While devastation sweeps along the plain:
Nor shall the child of poverty despair,

---

*Inscribed on a stone in Euston Park wall.

But bless The Power that rules the changing year;
Assur'd,—though horrors round his cottage reign,—
That Spring will come, and Nature smile again.

WINTER

With kindred pleasures mov'd, and cares opprest,
Sharing alike our weariness and rest;
Who lives the daily partner of our hours
Through every change of heat, and frost, and show'rs,
Partakes our cheerful meals, partaking first
In mutual labour and fatigue and thirst;
The kindly intercourse will ever prove
A bond of amity and social love.
To more than man this generous warmth extends,
And oft the team and shiv'ring herd befriends;
Tender solicitude the bosom fills,
And Pity executes what Reason wills:
Youth learns compassion's tale from ev'ry tongue,
And flies to aid the helpless and the young.

   When now, unsparing as the scourge of war,
Blasts follow blasts, and groves dismantled roar,
Around their home the storm-pinch'd Cattle lows,
No nourishment in frozen pastures grows;
Yet frozen pastures every morn resound
With fair abundance thund'ring to the ground.
For though on hoary twigs no buds peep out,
And e'en the hardy brambles cease to sprout,
Beneath dread Winter's level sheets of snow
The sweet nutritious turnip deigns to grow.
Till now imperious want and wide-spread dearth
Bid Labour claim her treasure, from the earth,
On Giles, and such as Giles, the labour falls,
To strew the frequent load where hunger calls.
On driving gales sharp hail indignant flies,
And sleet, more irksome still, assails his eyes;
Snow clogs his feet; or if no snow is seen,
The field with all its juicy store to screen,
Deep goes the frost, till every root is found
A rolling mass of ice upon the ground.
No tender ewe can break her nightly fast,
Nor heifer strong begin the cold repast,
Till Giles with pond'rous beetle foremost go,
And scatt'ring splinters fly at every blow;
When pressing round him, eager for the prize,
From their mixt breath warm exhalations rise.

In beaded rows if drops now deck the spray,
While Phoebus grants a momentary ray,
Let but a cloud's broad shadow intervene,
And stiffen'd into gems the drops are seen;
And down the furrow'd oak's broad southern side
Streams of dissolving rime no longer glide.

Though Night approaching bids for rest prepare,
Still the flail echoes through the frosty air,
Nor stops till deepest shades of darkness come,
Sending at length the weary Labourer home.
From him, with bed and nightly food supplied,
Throughout the yard, hous'd round on every side,
Deep-plunging Cows their rustling feast enjoy,
And snatch sweet mouthfuls from the passing Boy,
Who moves unseen beneath his trailing load,
Fills the tall racks, and leaves a scatter'd road;
Where oft the swine from ambush warm and dry
Bolt out, and scamper headlong to their sty,
When Giles with well-known voice, already there,
Deigns them a portion of his evening care.

Him, though the cold may pierce, and storms molest,
Succeeding hours shall cheer with warmth and rest;
Gladness to spread, and raise the grateful smile,
He hurls the faggot bursting from the pile,
And many a log and rifted trunk conveys,
To heap the fire, and wide extend the blaze,
That quivering strong through every opening flies,
Whilst smoky columns unobstructed rise.
For the rude architect, unknown to fame,
(Nor symmetry nor elegance his aim)
Who spreads his floors of solid oak on high,
On beams rough-hewn, from age to age that lie,
Bade his wide fabric unimpair'd sustain
Pomona's store, and cheese, and golden grain;
Bade, from its central base, capacious laid,
The well-wrought chimney rear its lofty head;
Where since hath many a savoury ham been stor'd,
And tempests howl'd, and Christmas gambols roar'd.

Flat on the hearth the glowing embers lie,
And flames reflected dance in every eye:
There the long billet forced at last to bend,
While gushing sap froths out at either end,
Throws round its welcome heat:—the ploughman smiles,
And oft the joke runs hard on sheepish Giles,
Who sits joint tenant of the corner-stool,
The converse sharing, though in duty's school;
For now attentively 'tis his to hear
Interrogations from the Master's chair.

'Left ye your bleating charge, when day-light fled,
'Near where the hay-stack lifts its snowy head?
'Whose fence of bushy furze, so close and warm,
'May stop the slanting bullets of the storm.
'For, hark! it blows; a dark and dismal night:
'Heaven guide the trav'ller's fearful steps aright!
'Now from the woods, mistrustful and sharp-ey'd,
'The Fox in silent darkness seems to glide,
'Stealing around us, list'ning as he goes,
'If chance the Cock or stamm'ring Capon crows,
'Or Goose, or nodding Duck, should darkling cry,
'As if appriz'd of lurking danger nigh:
'Destruction waits them, Giles, if e'er you fail
'To bolt their doors against the driving gale.
'Strew'd you (still mindful of th' unshelter'd head)
'Burdens of straw, the cattle's welcome bed?
'Thine heart should feel, what thou may'st hourly see,
'That duty's basis is humanity.
'Of pain's unsavoury cup though thou may'st taste
'(The wrath of Winter from the black north-east,)
'Thine utmost suff'rings in the coldest day
'A period terminates, and joys repay.
'Perhaps e'en now, while here those joys we boast,
'Full many a bark rides down the neighb'ring coast,
'Where the high northern waves tremendous roar,
'Drove down by blasts from Norway's icy shore.
'The Sea-boy there, less fortunate than thou,
'Feels all thy pains in all the gusts that blow;
'His freezing hands now drench'd, now dry, by turns;
'Now lost, now seen, the distant light that burns,
'On some tall cliff uprais'd, a flaming guide,

'That throws its friendly radiance o'er the tide.
'His labours cease not with declining day,
'But toils and perils mark his wat'ry way;
'And whilst in peaceful dreams secure we lie,
'The ruthless whirlwinds rage along the sky,
'Round his head whistling;—and shalt thou repine,
'While this protecting roof still shelters thine!'

 Mild, as the vernal show'r, his words prevail,
And aid the moral precept of his tale:
His wond'ring hearers learn, and ever keep
These first ideas of the restless deep:
And, as the opening mind a circuit tries,
Present felicities in value rise.
Increasing pleasures every hour they find,
The warmth more precious, and the shelter kind;
Warmth that long reigning bids the eyelids close,
As through the blood its balmy influence goes,
When the cheer'd heart forgets fatigues and cares,
And drowsiness alone dominion bears.

 Sweet then the ploughman's slumbers, hale and young,
When the last topic dies upon his tongue;
Sweet then the bliss his transient dreams inspire,
Till chilblains wake him, or the snapping fire:

 He starts, and ever thoughtful of his team,
Along the glitt'ring snow a feeble gleam
Shoots from his lantern, as he yawning goes
To add fresh comforts to their night's repose;
Diffusing fragrance as their food he moves,
And pats the jolly sides of those he loves.
Thus full replenish'd, perfect ease possest,
From night till morn alternate food and rest,
No rightful cheer withheld, no sleep debarr'd,
Their each day's labour brings its sure reward.
Yet when from plough or lumb'ring cart set free,
They taste awhile the sweets of liberty:
E'en sober Dobbin lifts his clumsy heel
And kicks, disdainful of the dirty wheel;
But soon, his frolic ended, yields again
To trudge the road, and wear the clinking chain.

Short-sighted Dobbin!—thou canst only see
The trivial hardships that encompass thee:
Thy chains were freedom, and thy toils repose:
Could the poor post-horse tell thee all his woes;
Show thee his bleeding shoulders, and unfold
The dreadful anguish he endures for gold:
Hir'd at each call of business, lust, or rage,
That prompts the trav'ller on from stage to stage.
Still on his strength depends their boasted speed;
From them his limbs grow weak, his bare ribs bleed;
And though he groaning quickens at command,
Their extra shilling in the rider's hand
Becomes his bitter scourge,—'tis he must feel
The double effects of the lash and steel;
Till when, up hill, the destin'd inn he gains,
And trembling under complicated pains,
Prone from his nostrils, darting on the ground,
His breath emitted floats in clouds around:
Drops chase each other down his chest and sides,
And spatter'd mud his native colour hides:
Through his swoln veins the boiling torrent flows,
And every nerve a separate torture knows.
His harness loos'd, he welcomes, eager ey'd,
The pail's full draught that quivers by his side;
And joys to see the well-known stable door,
As the starv'd mariner the friendly shore.

Ah, well for him if here his suff'rings ceas'd,
And ample hours of rest his pains appeas'd!
But rous'd again, and sternly bade to rise,
And shake refreshing slumber from his eyes,
Ere his exhausted spirits can return,
Or through his frame reviving ardour burn,
Come forth he must, though limping, maim'd, and sore;
He hears the whip; the chaise is at the door:—
The collar tightens, and again he feels
His half-heal'd wounds inflam'd; again the wheels
With tiresome sameness in his ears resound,
O'er blinding dust, or miles of flinty ground.
Thus nightly robb'd, and injur'd day by day,
His piece-meal murd'rers wear his life away.
What say'st thou Dobbin? what though hounds await

(xii)   Edward Jenner discoverer of the small-pox vaccine

Reproduced by courtesy of the National Portrait Gallery, London

A VIEW NEAR BURY- SUFFOLK.

(xiii)   Cartoon of Capel Lofft which appeared in a Scrapbook, Bury and immediate inviro
published by S. Knight of London in the early 19th century

(xiv) Euston Hall, Suffolk home of the Duke of Grafton.

(xv) Church in Euston Park.

(xvi)   Memorial plaque to Trouncer in the Park wall of Euston Hall.

(xvii)   The cross-roads at Lanket's Grove looking towards the green where Bardwell Fair was formerly held.

(xviii) The gateway to Euston Park (above) and (xix) the nearby drove way and site of the stile, now replaced by the gate, which figure prominently in the poem *The Fakenham Ghost*.

(xx)　Lankets Grove.

(xxi) Barnham Water.

(xxii)   Head and foot stones in Honington Churchyard.
From left Robert's father (footstone), mother (headstone)
and his brother and sister-in-law (double headstone).

(xxiii)   Robert Bloomfield's headstone (left)
on his grave in the church yard at Campton.

With open jaws the moment of thy fate,
No better fate attends his public race;
His life is misery, and his end disgrace.
Then freely bear thy burden to the mill;
Obey but one short law,—thy driver's will.
Affection to thy memory ever true,
Shall boast of mighty loads that Dobbin drew;
And back to childhood shall the mind with pride
Recount thy gentleness in many a ride
To pond, or field, or Village-fair, when thou
Held'st high thy braided main and comely brow;
And oft the Tale shall rise to homely fame
Upon thy gen'rous spirit and thy name.

   Though faithful to a proverb we regard
The midnight Chieftain of the farmer's yard,
Beneath whose guardianship all hearts rejoice,
Woke by the echo of his hollow voice;
Yet as the Hound may falt'ring quit the pack,
Snuff the foul scent, and hasten yelping back;
And e'en the docile Pointer know disgrace,
Thwarting the gen'ral instinct of his race;
E'en so the Mastiff, or the meaner Cur,
At times will from the path of duty err,
(A pattern of fidelity by day,
By night a murderer, lurking for his prey,)
And round the pastures or the fold will creep,
And, coward-like attack the peaceful sheep.
Alone the wanton mischief he pursues,
Alone in reeking blood his jaws imbrues;
Chasing amain his frighten'd victims round,
Till death in wild confusion strews the ground;
Then wearied out, to kennel sneaks away,
And licks his guilty paws till break of day.

   The deed discover'd, and the news once spread,
Vengeance hangs o'er the unknown culprit's head:
And careful Shepherds extra hours bestow
In patient watchings for the common foe;
A foe most dreaded now, when rest and peace
Should wait the season of the flock's increase.

In part these nightly terrors to dispel,
Giles, ere he sleeps, his little flock must tell.
From the fire-side with many a shrug he hies,
Glad if the full-orb'd Moon salute his eyes,
And through th' unbroken stillness of the night
Shed on his path her beams of cheering light.
With saunt'ring step he climbs the distant stile,
Whilst all around him wears a placid smile;
There views the white-rob'd clouds in clusters driven,
And all the glorious pageantry of Heaven.
Low, on the utmost bound'ry of the sight.
The rising vapours catch the silver light;
Thence Fancy measures, as they parting fly,
Which first will throw its shadow on the eye,
Passing the source of light; and thence away,
Succeeded quick by brighter still than they.
Far yet above these wafted clouds are seen
(In a remoter sky, still more serene,)
Others, detach'd in ranges through the air,
Spotless as snow, and countless as they're fair;
Scatter'd immensely wide from east to west,
The beauteous 'semblance of a Flock at rest.
These, to the raptur'd mind, aloud proclaim
Their Mighty Shepherd's everlasting Name.

    Whilst thus the loit'rer's utmost stretch of soul
Climbs the still clouds, or passes those that roll,
And loos'd Imagination soaring goes
High o'er his home, and all his little woes,
Time glides away; neglected Duty calls;
At once from plains of light to earth he falls,
And down a narrow lane, well known by day,
With all his speed pursues his sounding way,
In thought still half absorb'd and chill'd with cold;
When lo! an object frightful to behold;
A grisly Spectre, cloth'd in silver-gray,
Around whose feet the waving shadows play,
Stands in his path!—He stops, and not a breath
Heaves from his heart, that sinks almost to death.
Loud the Owl halloos o'er his head unseen;
All else is silent, dismally serene:
Some prompt ejaculation, whisper'd low,

Yet bears him up against the threat'ning foe;
And thus poor Giles, though half inclined to fly,
Mutters his doubts, and strains his stedfast eye.
"'Tis not my crimes thou com'st here to reprove;
'No murders stain my soul, no perjur'd love;
'If thou'rt indeed what here thou seem'st to be,
'Thy dreadful mission cannot reach to me.
'By parents taught still to mistrust mine eyes,
'Still to approach each object of surprise,
'Lest Fancy's formful visions should deceive
'In moon-light paths, or glooms of falling eve,
'This then's the moment when my mind should try
'To scan thy motionless deformity;
'But oh, the fearful task! yet well I know
'An aged Ash, with many a spreading bough,
'(Beneath whose leaves I've found a Summer's bow'r,
'Beneath whose trunk I've weather'd many a show'r,)
'Stands singly down this solitary way,
'But far beyond where now my footsteps stay.
"'Tis true, thus far I've come with heedless haste;
'No reck'ning kept, no passing objects trac'd:—
'And can I then have reach'd that very tree?
'Or is its reverend form assum'd by thee?'
The happy thought alleviates his pain:
He creeps another step; then stops again;
Till slowly, as his noiseless feet draw near,
Its perfect lineaments at once appear;
Its crown of shiv'ring ivy whispering peace,
And its white bark that fronts the moon's pale face.
Now, whilst his blood mounts upward, now he knows
The solid gain from that conviction flows;
And strengthen'd Confidence shall hence fulfil
(With conscious Innocence more valued still)
The dreariest task that winter nights can bring,
By churchyard dark, or grove, or fairy ring;
Still buoying up the timid mind of youth,
Till loit'ring Reason hoists the scale of Truth.
With these blest guardians Giles his course pursues,
Till numbering his heavy-sided ewes,
Surrounding stillness tranquillize his breast,
And shape the dreams that wait his hours of rest.

As when retreating tempests we behold,
Whose skirts at length the azure sky unfold,
And full of murmurings and mingled wrath,
Slowly unshroud the smiling face of earth,
Bringing the bosom joy: so Winter flies!—
And see, the Source of Life and Light uprise!
A height'ning arch o'er southern hills he bends,
Warm on the cheek the slanting beam descends,
And gives the reeking mead a brighter hue,
And draws the modest primrose bud to view.
Yet frosts succeed, and winds impetuous rush,
And hail-storms rattle through the budding bush;
And night-fall'n Lambs require the shepherd's care,
And teeming Ewes, that still their burdens bear;
Beneath whose sides to-morrow's dawn may see
The milk-white strangers bow the trembling knee;
At whose first birth the powerful instinct's seen
That fills with champions the daisied green:
For Ewes that stood aloof with fearful eye,
With stamping foot now Men and Dogs defy,
And obstinately faithful to their young,
Guard their first steps to join the bleating throng.

But casualties and death from damps and cold
Will still attend the well-conducted fold:
Her tender offspring dead, the Dam aloud
Calls, and runs wild amidst th' unconscious crowd:
And orphan'd sucklings raise the piteous cry;
No wool to warm them, no defenders nigh.
And must her streaming milk then flow in vain?
Must unregarded innocence complain?
No;—ere this strong solicitude subside,
Maternal fondness may be fresh applied,
And the adopted stripling still may find
A parent most assiduously kind.
For this he's doom'd awhile disguis'd to range
(For fraud or force must work the wish'd-for change);
For this his predecessor's skin he wears,
Till, cheated into tenderness and cares,
The unsuspecting dam, contented grown,
Cherish and guard the fondlings as her own.

Thus all by turns to fair perfection rise;
Thus twins are parted to increase their size:
Thus instinct yields as interest points the way,
Till the bright flock, augmenting every day,
On sunny hills and vales of springing flow'rs
With ceaseless clamour greet the vernal hours.

The humbler Shepherd here with joy beholds
Th' approv'd economy of crowded folds,
And, in his small contracted round of cares,
Adjusts the practice of each hint he hears;
For Boys with emulation learn to glow,
And boast their pastures, and their healthful show
Of well-grown Lambs, the glory of the spring;
And field to field in competition bring.

E'en Giles, for all his cares and watchings past,
And all his contests with the wintry blast,
Claims a full share of that sweet praise bestow'd
By gazing neighbours when along the road,
Or village green, his curly-coated throng
Suspends the chorus of the Spinner's song;
When Admiration's unaffected grace
Lisps from the tongue, and beams in ev'ry face:
Delightful moments!—Sunshine, Health and Joy,
Play round, and cheer the elevated Boy!
'Another Spring!' his heart exulting cries;
'Another Year!' with promis'd blessings rise!—
'Eternal Power! from whom those blessings flow,
'Teach me still more to wonder, more to know:
'Seed-time and Harvest let me see again;
'Wander the leaf-strewn wood, the frozen plain:
'Let the first flower, corn-waving field, plain, tree,
'Here round my home, still lift my soul to Thee;
'And let me ever, midst thy bounties, raise
'An humble note of thankfulness and praise!'—
April 22, 1798.

THE HORKEY

What gossips prattled in the sun,
Who talk'd him fairly down,
Up, Mem'ry! tell; 'tis Suffolk fun,
And lingo of their own.

Ah! Judie Twitchet! though thou'rt dead,
With thee the tale begins;
For still seems thrumming in my head
The rattling of thy pins.

Thou Queen of knitters! for a ball
Of worsted was thy pride;
With dangling stockings great and small,
And world of clack beside!

"We did so laugh; the moon shone bright;
"More fun you never knew;
"'Twas Farmer Cheerum's Horkey Night,
"And I, and Grace, and Sue——

"But bring a stool, sit round about,
"And boys be quiet, pray;
"And let me tell my story out;
"'Twas sitch a merry day!

"The butcher whistled at the door,
"And brought a load of meat;
"Boys rubb'd their hands, and cried, 'there's more!'
"Dogs wagg'd their tails to see 't.

"On went the boilers till the hake
"Had much ado to bear 'em;
"The magpie talk'd for talking' sake,
"Birds sung:—but who could hear 'em?

"Creak went the jack; the cats were scar'd,
"We had not time to heed 'em;
"The owd hins cackled in the yard,
"For we forgot to feed 'em!

"Yet 'twas not I, as I may say,
"Because as how, d'ye see,
"I only help'd there for the day;
"They cou'dn't lay't to me.

"Now Mrs. Cheerum's best lace cap
"Was mounted on her head,
"Guests at the door began to rap,
"And now the cloth was spread.

"Then clatter went the earthen plates—
" 'Mind, Judie,' was the cry;
"I could have cop't 'em at their pates;
" 'Trenchers for me,' said I,

"That look so clean upon the ledge,
"And never mind a fall;
"They never turn a sharp knife's edge;—
"But fashion rules us all.

"Home came the jovial Horkey load,
"Last of the whole year's crop;
"And Grace amongst the green boughs rode
"Right plump upon the top.

"This way and that the waggon reel'd,
"And never queen rode higher;
"Her cheeks were colour'd in the fields,
"And ours before the fire.

"The laughing harvest-folks, and John,
"Came in and look'd askew;
"'Twas my red face that set them on,
"And then they leer'd at Sue.

"And Farmer Cheerum went, good man,
"And broach'd the Horkey beer;
"And sitch a mort of folk began
"To eat up our good cheer.

"Says, he 'Thank God for what's before us;
"That thus we meet agen;'
"The mingling voices, like a chorus,
"Join'd cheerfully, 'Amen.'—

"Welcome and plenty, there they found 'em,
"The ribs of beef grew light;
"And puddings—till the boys got round 'em,
"And then they vanish'd quite!

"Now all the guests, with Farmer Crouder,
"Began to prate of corn;
"And we found out they talk'd the louder,
"The oft'ner pass'd the Horn.

"Out came the nuts; we set a cracking;
"The ale came round our way:
"By gom, we women fell a clacking
"As loud agoin as they.

"John sung 'Old Benbow' loud and strong,
"And I, 'The Constant Swain;'
" 'Cheer up, my Lads,' was Simon's song,
" 'We'll conquer them again.'

"Now twelve o'clock was drawing nigh,
"And all in merry cue;
"I knock'd the cask, 'O, ho!' said I,
" 'We've almost conquer'd you.'

"My Lord begg'd round, and held his hat,
"Says Farmer Gruff, says he,
" 'There's many a Lord, Sam, I know that,
" Has begg'd as well as thee.'

"Bump in his hat the shillings tumbled
"All round among the folks;
" 'Laugh if you wool,' said Sam, and mumbled,
" 'You pay for all your jokes.'

"Joint stock, you know, among the men,
"To drink at their own charges;
"So up they got full drive, and then
"Went out to halloo largess!

112

"And sure enough the noise they made!!—
—"But let me mind my tale:
"We follow'd them, we worn't afraid,
"We'ad all been drinking ale.

"As they stood hallooing back to back,
"We, lightly as a feather,
"Went sideling round, and in a crack
"Had pinn'd their coats together.

"'Twas near upon't as light as noon;
" 'A largess,' on the hill,
"They shouted to the full round moon,
"I think I hear 'em still!

"But when they found the trick, my stars!
"They well knew who to blame,
"Our giggles turn'd to loud ha, ha's,
"And arter us they came.

"The hindmost was the dairy-maid,
"And Sam came blundering by;
"She could not shun him, so they said;
"I know she did not try.

"Sue round the neat-house squalling ran,
"Where Simon scarcely dare;
"He stopt,—for he's a fearful man—
" ' By gom there's suffen there.'

"And off set John, with all his might,
"To chase me down the yard,
"Till I was nearly gran'd outright;
"He hugg'd so woundy hard.

"Still they kept up the race and laugh,
"And round the house we flew;
"But hark ye! the best fun by half
"Was Simon arter Sue.

"She car'd not, dark nor light, not she,
"So, near the dairy door
"She pass'd a clean white hog you see,
"They'd kilt the day before.

"High on the spirket there it hung,—
" 'Now, Susie—what can save ye?'
"Round the cold pig his arms he flung,
"And cried, 'Ah! here I have ye!'

"The farmers heard what Simon said,
"And what a noise! good lack!
"Some almost laugh'd themselves to dead,
"And others clapt his back.

"We all at once began to tell
"What fun we had abroad;
"But Simon stood our jeers right well;
—"He fell asleep and snor'd.

"Then in his button-hole upright,
"Did Farmer Crouder put
"A slip of paper, twisted tight,
"And held the candle to't.

"It smok'd, and smok'd, beneath his nose,
"The harmless blaze crept higher;
"Till with a vengeance up he rose,
"Grace, Judie, Sue! fire, fire!

"The clock struck one—some talk'd of parting,
"Some said it was a sin,
"And hitch'd their chairs;—but those for starting
"Now let the moonlight in.

"Owd women, loitering for the nonce,
"Stood praising the fine weather;
"The menfolks took the hint at once
"To kiss them altogether.

"And out ran every soul beside,
"A shanny-pated crew;
"Owd folks could neither run nor hide,
"So some ketch'd one, some tew.

"They skriggl'd and began to scold,
"But laughing got the master;
"Some quack'ling cried, 'let go your hold;'
"The farmers held the faster.

"All innocent, that I'll be sworn,
"There worn't a bit of sorrow,
"And women, if their gowns are torn,
"Can mend them on the morrow.

"Our shadows helter skelter danc'd
"About the moonlight ground;
"The wondering sheep, as on we pranc'd,
"Got up and gaz'd around.

"And well they might—till Farmer Cheerum,
"Now with a hearty glee,
"Bade all good morn as he came near 'em,
"And then to bed went he.

"Then off we stroll'd this way and that,
"With merry voices ringing;
"And Echo answer'd us right pat,
"As home we rambled singing.

"For, when we laugh'd, it laugh'd again,
"And to our own doors follow'd!
" 'Yo, ho!' we cried; 'Yo, ho!' so plain,
"The misty meadow halloo'd.

"That's all my tale, and all the fun,
"Come, turn your wheels about;
"My worsted, see!—that's nicely done,
"Just held my story out!!"

Poor Judie!—Thus Time knits or spins
    The worsted from Life's ball!
Death stopt thy tales, and stopt thy pins,
—And so he'll serve us all.

. . . .

hake — a sliding pot-hook,   copt — thrown,
sitch a mort — such a number,   Lord — the leader of the
reapers,   neat-house — cow house,   suffen — something,
graned — strangled,   sperket — iron hook,   for the nonce —
for the purpose,   shanny-pated — giddy, thoughtless,
skriggled — struggled quickly,   quackling — choking.

MY OLD OAK TABLE

Friend of my peaceful days, substantial friend,
Whom wealth can never change, nor int'rest bend,
I love thee like a child. Thou wert to me
The dumb companion of my misery,
And oft'ner of my joys;—then as I spoke,
I shar'd thy sympathy, Old Heart of Oak!
For surely when my labour ceas'd at night,
With trembling, feverish hands, and aching sight,
The draught that cheer'd me and subdu'd my care,
On thy broad shoulders thou wert proud to bear.
O'er thee, with expectation's fire elate,
I've sat and ponder'd on my future fate:
On thee, with winter muffins for thy store,
I've lean'd, and quite forgot that I was poor.

Where dropp'd the acorn that gave birth to thee?
Can'st thou trace back thy line of ancestry?
We're match'd old friend, and let us not repine,
Darkness o'erhangs thy origin and mine;
Both may be truly honourable: yet,
We'll date our honours from the day we met;
When, of my worldly wealth the parent stock,
Right welcome up the Thames from Woolwich Dock
Thou cam'st, when hopes ran high and love was young;
But soon our olive-branches round thee sprung;
Soon came the days that tried a faithful wife,
The noise of children and the cares of life.
Then, midst the threat'nings of a wintry sky,
That cough which blights the bud of infancy,
The dread of parents, Rest's inveterate foe,
Came like a plague, and turn'd my songs to woe.

Rest! without thee, what strength can long survive?
What spirit keep the flame of Hope alive?
The midnight murmur of the cradle gave
Sounds of despair, and chilly as the grave
We felt its undulating blast arise,
Midst whisper'd sorrows and ten thousand sighs.

Expiring embers warn'd us each to sleep,
By turns to watch alone, by turns to weep,
By turns to hear, and keep from starting wild,
The sad, faint wailings of a dying child.
But Death, obedient to Heav'n's high command,
Withdrew his jav'lin, and unclench'd his hand;
The little sufferers triumph'd over pain,
Their mother smil'd, and bade me hope again.
Yet Care gain'd ground, Exertion triumph'd less,
Thick fell the gathering terrors of Distress;
Anxiety and Griefs without a name,
Had made their dreadful inroads on my frame;
The creeping Dropsy, cold as cold could be,
Unnerv'd my arm, and bow'd my head to thee.
Thou to thy trust, old friend, hast not been true;
These eyes the bitterest tears they ever knew
Let fall upon thee; now all wip'd away;
But what from mem'ry shall wipe out that day?
The great, the wealthy of my native land,
To whom a guinea is a grain of sand,
I thought upon them, for my thoughts were free,
But all unknown were then my woes and me.

Still, Resignation was my dearest friend,
And Reason pointed to a glorious end;
With anxious sighs, a parent's hopes and pride,
I wish'd to live—I trust I could have died!
But winter's clouds pursu'd their stormy way,
And March brought sunshine with the length'ning day,
And bade my heart arise, that morn and night
Now throbb'd with irresistible delight.
Delightful 'twas to leave disease behind,
And feel the renovation of the mind!
To lead abroad, upborne on Pleasure's wing,
Our children, midst the glories of the spring;
Our fellow-sufferers, our only wealth,
To gather daisies in the breeze of health!

'Twas then, too, when our prospects grew so fair,
And Sabbath bells announc'd the morning pray'r;
Beneath that vast gigantic dome we bow'd,
That lifts its flaming cross above the cloud;

Had gain'd the centre of the chequer'd floor;—
That instant, with reverberating roar,
Burst forth the pealing organ—mute we stood,
The strong sensation boiling through my blood,
Rose in a storm of joy, allied to pain,
I wept, and worshipp'd God, and wept again;
And felt, amidst the fervour of my praise,
The sweet assurances of better days.

In that gay season, honest friend of mine,
I mark'd the brilliant sun upon thee shine;
Imagination took her flights so free,
Home was delicious with my book and thee;
The purchas'd nosegay, or brown ears of corn,
Were thy gay plumes upon a summer's morn,
Awakening memory, that disdains control,
They spoke the darling language of my soul;
They whisper'd tales of joy, of peace, of truth,
And conjur'd back the sunshine of my youth.
Fancy presided at the joyful birth,
I pour'd the torrent of my feelings forth;
Conscious of truth in Nature's humble track,
And wrote "The Farmer's Boy" upon thy back!
Enough, old friend:—thou'rt mine; and shalt partake,
While I have pen to write, or tongue to speak,
Whatever fortune deals me.—Part with thee?
No, not till death shall set my spirit free;
For know, should plenty crown my life's decline,
A most important duty may be thine:
Then, guard me from Temptation's base control,
From apathy and littleness of soul:
The sight of thy old frame, so rough, so rude,
Shall twitch the sleeve of nodding Gratitude;
Shall teach me but to venerate the more
Honest Oak Tables and their guests—the poor;
Teach me unjust distinctions to deride,
And falsehoods gender'd in the brain of Pride;
Shall give to Fancy still the cheerful hour,
To Intellect, its freedom and its power;
To Hospitality's enchanting ring
A charm, which nothing but thyself can bring.
The man who would not look with honest pride

On the tight bark that stemm'd the roaring tide,
And bore him, when he bow'd the trembling knee,
Home, through the mighty perils of the sea,
I love him not.—He ne'er shall be my guest;
Nor sip my cup, nor witness how I'm blest;
Nor lean to bring my honest friend to shame,
A sacrilegious elbow on thy frame;
But thou through life a monitor shalt prove,
Sacred to Truth, to Poetry, and Love.

RICHARD AND KATE:

OR

FAIR-DAY

A SUFFOLK BALLAD

'Come, Goody, stop your humdrum wheel,
'Sweep up your orts, and get your hat;
'Old joys reviv'd once more I feel,
''Tis Fair-day;—ay, and more than that.

'Have you forgot, Kate, prithee say,
'How many Seasons here we've tarried?
''Tis forty years, this very day,
'Since you and I, old Girl, were married!

'Look out;—the Sun shines warm and bright,
'The Stiles are low, the Paths all dry;
'I know you cut your corns last night:
'Come; be as free from care as I.

'For I'm resolved once more to see
'That place where we so often met;
'Though few have had more cares than we,
'We've none just now to make us fret.'

Kate scorn'd to damp the generous flame
That warm'd her aged Partner's breast:
Yet, ere determination came,
She thus some trifling doubts express'd:

'Night will come on; when seated snug,
'And you've perhaps begun some tale,
'Can you then leave your dear stone mug;
'Leave all the folks and all the ale?'

'Ay, Kate, I wool;—because I know,
'Though time has been we both could run,
'Such days are gone and over now;—
'I only mean to see the fun.'

120

She straight slipp'd off the Wall, and Band,
And laid aside her Lucks and Twitches:
And to the Hutch she reach'd her hand,
And gave him out his Sunday Breeches.

His Mattock he behind the door
And Hedging-gloves again replac'd;
And look'd across the yellow Moor,
And urg'd his tottering Spouse to haste.

The day was up, the air serene,
The Firmament without a cloud;
The Bee humm'd o'er the level green,
Where knots of trembling Cowslips bow'd.

And Richard thus, with heart elate,
As past things rush'd across his mind,
Over his shoulder talk'd to Kate,
Who, snug tuckt up, walk'd slow behind.

'When once a giggling Mawther you,
'And I a red-fac'd chubby Boy,
'Sly tricks you play'd me not a few;
'For mischief was your greatest joy.

'Once passing by this very Tree,
'A Gotch of Milk I'd been to fill,
'You shoulder'd me; then laugh'd to see
'Me and my Gotch spin down the Hill.'

''Tis true,' she said; 'But here behold,
'And marvel at the course of Time;
'Though you and I are both grown old,
'This Tree is only in its prime!'

'Well, Goody, don't stand preaching now;
'Folks don't preach Sermons at a Fair:
'We've rear'd Ten Boys and Girls you know;
'And I'll be bound they'll all be there.'

Now friendly nods and smiles had they,
From many a kind Fair-going face:
And many a pinch Kate gave away,
While Richard kept his usual pace.

At length arriv'd amidst the throng,
Grand-children bawling hemm'd them round;
And dragg'd them by the skirts along
Where gingerbread bestrew'd the ground.

And soon the aged couple spy'd
Their lusty Sons and Daughters dear:—
When Richard thus exulting cried,
'Didn't I tell you they'd be here?'

The cordial greetings of the soul
Were visible in every face:
Affection, void of all control,
Govern'd with a resistless grace.

'Twas good to see the honest strife,
Which should contribute most to please;
And hear the long recounted life,
Of infant tricks, and happy days.

But now, as at some nobler places,
Amongst the Leaders 'twas decreed
Time to begin the Dicky Races;
More fam'd for laughter than for speed.

Richard look'd on with wond'rous glee
And prais'd the Lad who chanc'd to win;
'Kate wa'nt I such a one as he?
'As like him, ay, as pin to pin?

'Full Fifty years are pass'd away
'Since I rode this same ground about:
'Lord, I was lively as the day!
'I won the High-lows out and out!

'I'm surely growing young again:
'I feel myself so kedge and plump.
'From head to foot I've not one pain;
'Nay hang me if I cou'dnt jump.'

Thus spoke the Ale in Richard's pate,
A very little made him mellow;
But still he lov'd his faithful Kate,
Who whisper'd thus, 'My good old fellow,

'Remember what you promis'd me:
'And see, the Sun is getting low;
'The Children want an hour, ye see,
'To talk a bit before we go.'

Like youthful Lover most complying
He turn'd, and chuckt her by the chin:
Then all across the green grass hieing,
Right merry faces, all akin.

Their farewell quart, beneath a tree
That droop'd its branches from above;
Awak'd the pure felicity
That waits upon Parental Love.

Kate view'd her blooming Daughters round,
And Sons who shook her wither'd hand:
Her features spoke what joy she found;
But utterance had made a stand.

The Children toppled on the green,
And bowl'd their fairings down the hill;
Richard with pride beheld the scene,
Nor could he for his life sit still.

A Father's uncheck'd feelings gave
A tenderness to all he said;
'My Boys, how proud am I to have
'My name thus round the country spread!

'Through all my days I've labour'd hard,
'And could of pains and crosses tell;
'But this is Labour's great reward,
'To meet ye thus, and see ye well.

'My good old Partner, when at home,
'Sometimes with wishes mingles tears;
'Goody,' says I, 'let what wool come,
'We've nothing for them but our pray'rs.

'May you be all as old as I,
'And see your sons to manhood grow;
'And, many a time before you die,
'Be just as pleas'd as I am now.'

Then, (raising still his Mug and voice,)
'An Old Man's weakness don't despise!
'I love you well, my Girls and Boys;
'God bless you all;'—so said his eyes—

For as he spoke, a big round drop
Fell, bounding on his ample sleeve;
A witness which he could not stop,
A witness which all hearts believe.

Thou, Filial Piety, wert there;
And round the ring, benignly bright,
Dwelt in the luscious half-shed tear,
And in the parting word—Good Night!

With thankful Hearts and strengthen'd Love,
The poor old Pair, supremely blest,
Saw the Sun sink behind the grove,
And gain'd once more their lowly rest.

BARNHAM WATER

Fresh from the Hall of Bounty sprung,
With glowing heart and ardent eye,
With song and rhyme upon my tongue,
And fairy visions dancing by,
The mid-day sun in all his pow'r
The backward valley painted gay;
Mine was a road without a flow'r,
Where one small streamlet cross'd the way.

What was it rous'd my soul to love?
What made the simple brook so dear?
It glided like the weary dove,
And never brook seem'd half so clear.
Cool pass'd the current o'er my feet,
Its shelving brink for rest was made,
But every charm was incomplete,
For Barnham Water wants a shade.

There, faint beneath the fervid sun,
I gaz'd in ruminating mood;
For who can see the current run
And snatch no feast of mental food?
"Keep pure thy soul," it seem'd to say,
"Keep that fair path by wisdom trod,
"That thou may'st hope to wind thy way,
"To fame worth boasting, and to God."

Long and delightful was the dream,
A waking dream that Fancy yields,
Till with regret I left the stream,
And plung'd across the barren fields;
To where of old rich abbeys smil'd
In all the pomp of gothic taste,
By fond tradition proudly styl'd,
The mighty "City in the East."

Near, on a slope of burning sand,
The shepherd boys had met to play,
To hold the plains at their command,
And mark the trav'ller's leafless way.

The trav'ller with a cheerful look
Would every pining thought forbear,
If boughs but shelter'd Barnham brook
He'd stop and leave his blessing there.

The Danish mounds of partial green,
Still, as each mouldering tower decays,
Far o'er the bleak unwooded scene
Proclaim their wond'rous length of days.
My burning feet, my aching sight,
Demanded rest,—why did I weep?
The moon arose, and such a night!
Good Heav'n! it was a sin to sleep.

All rushing came thy hallow'd sighs,
Sweet Melancholy, from my breast;
" 'Tis here that eastern greatness lies,
"That Might, Renown, and Wisdom rest!
"Here funeral rites the priesthood gave
"To chiefs who sway'd prodigious powers,
"The Bigods and the Mowbrays brave,
"From Framlingham's imperial towers."

Full of the mighty deeds of yore,
I bade good night the trembling beam;
Fancy e'en heard the battle's roar,
Of what but slaughter could I dream?
Bless'd be that night, that trembling beam,
Peaceful excursions Fancy made;
All night I heard the bubbling stream,
Yet Barnham Water wants a shade.

Whatever hurts my country's fame,
When wits and mountaineers deride,
To me grows serious, for I name
My native plains and streams with pride.
No mountain charms have I to sing,
No loftier minstrel's rights invade;
From trifles oft my raptures spring;
—Sweet Barnham Watèr wants a shade.

MARKET NIGHT

'O Winds, howl not so long and loud;
'Nor with your vengeance arm the snow:
'Bear hence each heavy-loaded cloud:
'And let the twinkling Star-beams glow.

'Now sweeping floods rush down the slope,
'Wide scattering ruin—Stars, shine soon!
'No other light my Love can hope;
'Midnight will want the joyous Moon.

'O guardian Spirits!—Ye that dwell
'Where woods, and pits, and hollow ways,
'The lone night trav'ller's fancy swell
'With fearful tales, of older days,—

'Press round him: guide his willing steed
'Through darkness, dangers, currents, snows;
'Wait where, from shelt'ring thickets freed,
'The dreary Heath's rude whirlwind blows;

'That o'er the Hill with furious sweep
'Now writhes, now rends the shiv'ring tree—
'Sure-footed beast, thy road thou'lt keep:
'Nor storm nor darkness startles thee:

'O blest assurance, (trusty steed,)
'To thee the buried road is known:
'Home, all the spur thy footsteps need,
'When loose the frozen rein is thrown.

'Between the roaring blasts that shake
'The naked Elder at the door,
'Though not one prattler to me speak,
'Their sleeping sighs delight me more.

'Sound is their rest:—they little know
'What pain, what cold, their Father feels:
'But dream, perhaps, they see him now,
'While each the promis'd Orange peels.

'Would it were so!—the fire burns bright,
'And on the warming trencher gleams;
'In Expectation's raptur'd sight
'How precious his arrival seems!

'I'll look abroad!—'tis piercing cold!—
'How the bleak wind assails his breast!
'Yet there the parting clouds unfold;
'The storm is verging o'er the West.

'There shines a Star!—O welcome Sight!
'Through the thin vapours bright'ning still!
'Yet 'twas beneath the fairest night
'The murd'rer stain'd yon lonely Hill.

'Mercy, kind Heav'n! such thoughts dispel!
'No voice, no foot is heard around!
'Perhaps he's near the haunted Well!
'But, Dapple knows each inch of ground.

'Distressing hour! uncertain fate!
'O Mercy, Mercy, guide him home!—
'Hark!—then I heard the distant gate,—
'Repeat it, Echo; quickly, come!

'One minute now will ease my fears—
'Or, still more wretched must I be?
'No: surely Heaven has spar'd our tears:
'I see him, cloth'd in snow;—'tis he.—

'Where have you stay'd? put down your load.
'How have you borne the storm, the cold?
'What horrors did I not forbode!—
'That Beast is worth his weight in gold.'

Thus spoke the joyful Wife;—then ran
In grateful steams to hide her head:
Dapple was hous'd, the weary Man
With joy glanc'd o'er the Children's bed.

'What, all asleep! —so best;' he cried;
'O what a night I've travell'd through!
'Unseen, unheard, I might have died;
'But Heav'n has brought me safe to you.

'Dear Partner of my nights and days,
'That smile becomes thee!—Let us then
'Learn, though mishap may cross our ways,
'It is not ours to reckon when.'

SONG

A HIGHLAND DROVER

RETURNING FROM ENGLAND

Now fare-thee-well, England: no further I'll roam;
But follow my shadow that points the way home:
Your gay southern shores shall not tempt me to stay;
For my Maggy's at home and my Children at play!
'Tis this makes my bonnet sit light on my brow,
Gives my sinews their strength and my bosom its glow.

Farewell, Mountaineers! my companions, adieu;
Soon, many long miles when I'm sever'd from you,
I shall miss your white Horns on the brink of the burn,
And o'er the rough Heaths, where you'll never return;
But in brave English pastures you cannot complain,
While your Drover speeds back to his Maggy again.

O Tweed! gentle Tweed, as I pass your green vales,
More than life, more than Love, my tir'd Spirit inhales;
There Scotland, my darling, lies full in my view,
With her bare-footed Lasses and Mountains so blue;
To the mountains away; my heart bounds like the hind;
For home is so sweet, and my Maggy so kind.

As day after day I still follow my course,
And in fancy trace back ev'ry Stream to its source,
Hope cheers me up hills, where the road lies before,
O'er hills just as high, and o'er tracks of wild Moor;
The keen polar Star nightly rising to view;
But Maggy's my Star, just as steady and true.

O Ghosts of my Fathers! O heroes, look down!
Fix my wand'ring thoughts on your deeds of renown;
For the glory of Scotland reigns warm in my breast,
And fortitude grows both from toil and from rest;
May your deeds and your worth be for ever in view,
And may Maggy bear sons not unworthy of you.

Love, why do you urge me, so weary and poor?
I cannot step faster, I cannot do more:
I've pass'd silver Tweed; e'en the Tay flows behind:
Yet fatigue I'll disdain;—my reward I shall find;
Thou, sweet smile of innocence, thou art my prize;
And the joy that will sparkle in Maggy's blue eyes.

She'll watch to the southward;—perhaps she will sigh,
That the way is so long, and the Mountains so high;
Perhaps some huge rock in the dusk she may see,
And will say in her fondness, 'That surely is he!'
Good Wife, you're deceiv'd; I'm still far from my home;
Go, sleep, my dear Maggy,—to-morrow I'll come.

THE FAKENHAM GHOST

A BALLAD

The Lawns were dry in Euston Park;
(Here Truth inspires my Tale;)
The lonely footpath, still and dark,
Led over Hill and Dale.

Benighted was an ancient Dame,
And fearful haste she made
To gain the vale of Fakenham,
And hail its Willow shade.

Her footsteps knew no idle stops,
But follow'd faster still;
And echo'd to the darksome Copse
That whisper'd on the Hill;

Where clam'rous Rooks, yet scarcely hush'd,
Bespoke a peopled shade;
And many a wing the foliage brush'd,
And hov'ring circuits made.

The dappled herd of grazing Deer
That sought the Shades by day,
Now started from her path with fear,
And gave the Stranger way.

Darker it grew; and darker fears
Came o'er her troubled mind;
When now, a short quick step she hears
Come patting close behind.

She turn'd; it stopt!—nought could she see
Upon the gloomy plain!
But, as she strove the Sprite to flee,
She heard the same again.

Now terror seiz'd her quaking frame:
For, where the path was bare,
The trotting Ghost kept on the same!
She mutter'd many a pray'r.

Yet once again, amidst her fright,
She tried what sight could do;
When through the cheating glooms of night,
A Monster stood in view.

Regardless of whate'er she felt,
It follow'd down the plain!
She own'd her sins, and down she knelt,
And said her pray'rs again.

Then on she sped; and Hope grew strong,
The white park-gate in view;
Which pushing hard, so long it swung,
That Ghost and all pass'd through.

Loud fell the gate against the post!
Her heart-strings like to crack:
For, much she fear'd the grisly Ghost
Would leap upon her back.

Still on, pat, pat, the Goblin went,
As it had done before:—
Her strength and resolution spent,
She fainted at the door.

Out came her Husband, much surpris'd:
Out came her Daughter dear:
Good-natur'd souls! all unadvis'd
Of what they had to fear.

The Candle's gleam pierc'd through the night,
Some short space o'er the green;
And there the little trotting Sprite
Distinctly might be seen.

An Ass's Foal had lost its Dam
Within the spacious Park;
And, simple as the playful Lamb,
Had follow'd in the dark.

No Goblin he; no imp of sin:
No crimes had ever known.
They took the shaggy stranger in,
And rear'd him as their own.

His little hoofs would rattle round
Upon the Cottage floor;
The Matron learn'd to love the sound
That frighten'd her before.

A favourite the Ghost became;
And, 'twas his fate to thrive:
And long he liv'd and spread his fame,
And kept the joke alive.

For many a laugh went through the Vale;
And some conviction too:—
Each thought some other Goblin tale,
Perhaps, was just as true.

IRISH NEWS

Tune: The Yorkshireman

From Dublin, ahoi! full of wonder and gazing,
I'm writing to you, brother Pat;
I've heard of a story so strange and amazing.
I'll talk about nothing but that:
I've heard of the queer little peaceable pimple,
That makes in the word such a row!
You might think all the doctors are crazy, or simple,
For they're all fell in love with the cow.

John Bull, though he holds us so tight in his tether,
Determined to give us relief,—
So he sends us this pimple, and Bedford together
—A glorious fellow for beef!—
And sure of the Fiend that makes holes in our faces,
He swears he can rid us all now;
So the sweet little milk-maids are sure of their graces,
And the farmer's in love with the cow.

In lectures galvanic, the world in a panic,
Beheld an ox-cheek twist about;
With frogs set a crawling and rabbits a squalling,
And sheep's heads that turned up the snout.
But what is all that, by my soul, brother Pat,
To the news that I'm telling you now?
New lectures are teaching, and parsons are preaching,
Ay, the parson's in love with the cow.

I'll tell you, moreover, how good neighbour Bull,
The scheme has so charmingly plann'd;
That by hook or by crook, he has got in his book,
The biggest great names in the land.
Yet some write and rave, that the pimple won't save,
And they prove it, I can't tell you how;
But while time lays them flat, let's remember, dear Pat,
That the world is in love with the cow.

Then what will we do, brother Pat, with the man
Who found out this glorious rig?
Sure, we'll gather him shamrocks as fast as we can,
And stick full every curl in his wig.
And may Unanimity, Concord, and Joy,
To the end of the world from just now,
Distinguish Humanity's heroes, my boy!
—Long life to John Bull and his cow!

From JOURNEY DOWN THE WYE

THE CORACLE

Pure temperate joys, and calm, were these;
We toss'd upon no Indian seas;
No savage chiefs, with tawny crew,
Came jabbering in the bark canoe
Our strength to dare, our course to turn;
Yet boats a South Sea chief would burn
Sculked in the alder shade. Each bore,
Devoid of keel, or sail or oar,
An upright fisherman, with eye
Of Brahmin-like solemnity;
Who scanned the surface either way,
And cleaved it like a fly at play;
And crossways bore a balanced pole,
To drive the salmon from his hole;
Then heedful leap'd, without parade,
On shore, as luck or fancy bade;
And o'er his back, in gallant trim,
Swung the light shell that carried him;
Then down again his burden threw,
And launched his whirling bowl anew;
Displaying, in his bow'ry station,
The infancy of navigation.

GLEANER'S SONG

Dear Ellen, your tales are all plenteously stored
With the joys of some bride, and the wealth of her lord:
    Of her chariots and dresses,
    And worldly caresses,
And servants that fly when she's waited upon:
But what can she boast if she weds unbeloved?
Can she e'er feel the joy that one morning I proved,
When I put on my new-gown and waited for John.

These fields, my dear Ellen, I knew them of yore,
Yet to me they ne'er looked so enchanting before;
    The distant bells ringing,
    The birds round us singing,
For pleasure is pure when affection is won;
They told me the troubles and cares of a wife;
But I loved him, and that was the pride of my life
When I put on my new-gown and waited for John.

He shouted and ran, as he leapt from the stile;
And what in my bosom was passing the while?
    For love knows the blessing
    Of ardent caressing,
When virtue inspires us and doubts are all gone.
The sunshine of Fortunes you say is divine;
True love and the sunshine of Nature were mine,
When I put on my new-gown and waited for John.

THE MAN IN THE MOON

The man in the moon looked down one night
Where a lad and his lass were walking;
Thinks he there must be very huge delight
In this kissing and nonsense-talking:
And so there must ('tis a well known case),
For it lasts both late and early.
So they talked him down, till he cover'd his face,
—They tired his patience fairly.

Then up rose the sun in his morning beams
And push'd back his nightcap to greet them.
Says he,—"As you boast of your darts and flames,
My darts and my flames shall meet them."
He scorch'd them both through the livelong day,
But they never once seem'd to mind him,
But laughed outright, as he skulk'd away,
And left a dark world behind him.

Then the man in the moon look'd down in a pet,
And said, "I believe I can cure you;
Though my brother has fail'd I may conquer yet—
If not I must try to endure you.
"Go home," he cried, "and attend to my rules,
And banish all thoughts of sorrow;
Then jump into bed you couple of fools,
And you'll both be wiser tomorrow."

ON REPAIRING A MINIATURE BUST OF
BUONAPARTE FOR MRS. PALMER

Madam:

E'en Lodi's stream, Marengo's plain
Amidst their heaps of dead,
Still left the illustrious Corsican
His laurels and his head.

What have you done? Was it to show
Still dire events portending,
That man may look as pure as snow,
Yet stand in need of mending.

Though mending is in part my trade,
When step by step I'm led on,
I ne'er the bold attempt yet made
To set a great man's head on.

But satirists may well suspect
That some great heads have long
Been our sole care, and (from neglect)
That we have set them wrong.

But jokes apart, 'tis plain to all,
Who see this broken bust,
The head of the original
Was rightly placed at first (fust).

SONNET

(To 15 gnats dancing in the sunbeams on Jan 3)

Welcome ye little fools, to cheer us now,
With recollection of a summer's eve;
And, though my heart cannot the cheat believe,
Still merrily dance about your leafless bough.
—I love you from my soul; and though I know
Ye can but die—to think how soon, I grieve;—
Perhaps to-night the blast of death may blow;
Frost be at hand—who grants you no reprieve.
—Your company's too small, I ween, that you
Thus raise the shrill note of your summer's song;
Yet dance away—'tis thus that children do,—
And wiser men to life's end dance along.
Die little gnats, as winds or frosts ordain:—
Death is our frost too—but we fly again.

LETTER 15

FROM A SWALLOW IN THE SOUTH OF FRANCE TO AN ENGLISH ROBIN

Dear Little Bob,

I remember your peaceful singing on the top of your shed, near my late dwelling, and I remember, also, that I promised to write you some account of my journey. You may recollect that at the close of your summer, when the flies became scarce, we all assembled on the roof of the highest building in the village, and talked loudly of the flight we intended to take. At last came the day appointed, and we mounted up in a vast body and steered southward. Being hatched in England, I had thought your valleys and streams matchless in beauty; but I am now a traveller, and have a traveller's privilege to say what I like. When we reach the great water, I was astonished at its width, but more still to see many travelling houses going at a prodigious rate, and sending forth from iron chimneys, columns of black smoke over the face of the water, reaching further than you ever flew in your life; they have a contrivance on each side which puts the waves all in commotion, but they are not wings. My mother says that in old times, when swallows came to England, there were no such things to be seen. We crossed this water and a fine sunny country beyond it, until I was tired, and we now found flies more abundant, though the oldest amongst us assure me that we must travel further still, over another wide water, into a country where men's faces are of the same colour as my feathers, black and tawny; but travellers are strange things. When I come to England again, I will endeavour to find your village. I hope, for your sake, you may have a mild winter and good lodgings.

This is all the news worth sending, and I must catch flies for myself now, you know.

So farewell,

for I am in haste.

HOB'S EPITAPH

A Grey-owl was I when on earth;
My master, a wondrous wise man,
Found out my deserts and my worth,
And would needs have me bred an exciseman.

He gave me the range of his house
And a favourite study, his shed,
Where I rush'd on the struggling mouse,
While science rush'd into my head.

In gauging, I still made advances:
Like schoolboy grew wiser and wiser;
Resolved in the world to take chances,
And try to come in supervisor.

But Fate comes, and Genius must fall:—
One morning, while gauging or drinking,
My wig overbalanced my tail,
And I found myself stifling and sinking.

Yet I died not like men—who still quarrel
Through life—yet to destiny yield:—
The tippler is drowned in his barrel;
The soldier is slain in the field.—

Not in love—nor in debt—nor in strife—
Nor in horrors attendant on war;—
In a barrel I gave up my life,
But mine was—a barrel of tar.

From HAZELWOOD HALL

GLEE FOR THREE VOICES
(Morrison, Emma and Mary)

"Love in a show'r safe shelter took
In a rosy bow'r beside a brook,
And wink'd and nodded with conscious pride
To his votaries drench'd on the other side;
"Come hither, sweet maids, there's a bridge below,
The toll-keeper, Hymen, will let you through—
      Come o'er the stream to me."

Then over they went in a huddle together,
Not caring much about wind or weather;
The bow'r was sweet, and the show'r was gone,
Again broke forth th' enlivening sun;
Some wish'd to return, but the toll-keeper said,
You're a wife now, lassy, I pass'd you a maid;
      Get back as you can for me!"

An extract from Act II Scene II in which the local squire, Morrison, Captain Goldhawk, and the wheelwright, Spokeum, engage in a witty and somewhat humorous dialogue, is typical of some of the other scenes in the play.

Spokeum is talking about his new invention—a machine to pick hops.

Morrison. I'll tell you what, neighbour Spokeum, it is much easier for fools to laugh at a proposed invention than to understand it when done.

Spokeum. Ay, sir, that's true enough: only that we projectors should not tell our secrets, I could show you the whole contrivance with seventeen wheels and——

Goldhawk. No, no, we don't wish to forestall you, or put you out of heart.

Morrison. Who have laughed at you most? Do I know any of the parties?

Spokeum. Why there is the thatcher, and he, you know, is a bit of a poet: he wants to set me about a contrivance to cut moonshine into slices. I don't know what to say to him; I am afraid he is too great a fool for anything.

142

Goldhawk.   Don't mind him, then; that is your only defence.

Spokeum.   But I have silenced another of my tormentors completely, by just turning round upon him with just a few words—You know the justice's clerk in the next village?

Morrison.   Know him, yes; he sets wheels to work too, but they will do more mischief than yours.

Spokeum.   Well, sir, he wanted to know if I could not invent a machine to make lawyers honest.

Goldhawk.   A very desirable thing, certainly.

Morrison.   And what could you say to him?

Spokeum.   O sir, very little, sir; but it came out in a minute—it came of itself. Says I, that machine has been invented long before we were born, and I have only to take pattern by one that has stood up on our common these forty years; it only consists of two, strong upright posts, with a cross bar at the top—you understand me gentlemen.

Goldhawk.   Why, Spokeum, you are a wit, and half a wag too, I perceive.

Spokeum.   Ay, sir, they all set up a loud laugh, not at "Old Hops" as they call me, but at the lawyer. I think I was "down upon him" there, as my father used to say.—Knock your foes down one at a time that's the way to settle them.

Morrison.   But what can you do when they make you angry? For all silly cunning-headed banterers try at that first.

Spokeum.   Sir, I defy them to make me angry, unless they speak slightingly of my son Joel; that I can't bear at all! Why, gentlemen, my son Joel and I, and your honours, are the cleverest men in these two parishes.

Goldhawk.   Thank you, Spokeum, for the honour you do us.

BETTY'S SONG

Come, John Gosling, put your Sunday clothes on;
Gladly shall I see you stump across the green,
And I'll sing, dear John, by the couch that you repose on,
And bring you such ale as was never, never seen.
     Come, lift the latch, John,
     Let me see your face;
And who shall be so happy and so blest as I and you!
     Here you'll see the leaves a shaking,
     Here you'll hear the pigs a squeaking;
Gobble, gobble, gobble, gobble; quack, quack, quack,
     And cock a doodle doo!
Round our farmyard yellow corn is growing,
Geese marching home with their cunning heads so high;
Down in the meads, John, there the cows are lowing;
The ducks in the pond, and the grunters in the sty,
     Come, lift the latch, John,
     Let me see your face;
And who shall be so happy and so blest as I and you
     Here you'll see the leaves a shaking,
     Here you'll hear the pigs a squeaking;
Gobble, gobble, gobble, gobble: quack, quack, quack,
     And cock a doodle doo!

THE VALE OF FAKENHAM

On thy calm joys with what delight I dream,
Thou dear green valley of my native stream!
Fancy o'er thee still waves th'enchanting wand,
And every nook of thine is fairy land.